LUIGI PIRANDELLO

Born in Sicily in 1867, Pirandello went to university in Palermo and Rome and took a doctorate in Bonn, before settling into the café-bohemian literary life of Rome in the 1890s. In 1894 he married the beautiful daughter of his father's business associate, but after bearing three children her already fragile mental stability was undermined by the financial ruin of both her father and her father-in-law. Pirandello supported his family by taking a university lecturing post – and by writing. Most of his best-known works were written in the shadows of his wife's increasingly dangerous condition, for which she was eventually committed to a mental clinic in 1919.

He first established his reputation with short stories, novels and two philosophical works. Playwriting came fairly late in his career, but it was his plays which won him an international reputation. Amongst his best known outside Italy are *Right You Are, If You Think So!* (1917), *The Rules of the Game* (1918), *Six Characters in Search of an Author* (1921), which provoked uproar when first staged in Rome but soon came to be seen as seminal, helped by an enormously successful production in Paris in 1924, *Naked* (1922), *Henry IV* (1922), *The Man with the Flower in his Mouth* (1923), *As You Desire Me* (1936) and *The Mountain Giants*, produced a year after his death in Rome in 1936. He won the Nobel Prize for Literature in 1934.

TANYA RONDER

Tanya Ronder trained at RADA and worked as an actress before turning to writing. Her other plays include adaptations of *Peribanez* by Lope de Vega and *Vernon God Little* by DBC Pierre, nominated for an Olivier Award for Best New Play (Young Vic); *Blood Wedding* and *Filumena* by Eduardo de Filippo (Almeida); Ionesco's *Macbett* (RSC); *Peter Pan* (Kensington Gardens, the O2 and USA tour); *Night Flight* (Muztheater, Amsterdam); *The Blake Diptych* (Fleur Darkin Ensemble) and the original play *Table* (National Theatre).

Her work for film includes *King Bastard*.

Luigi Pirandello

LIOLÀ

in a new version by
Tanya Ronder

NICK HERN BOOKS
London
www.nickhernbooks.co.uk

A Nick Hern Book

This version of *Liolà* first published in Great Britain as a paperback original in 2013 by Nick Hern Books Limited, The Glasshouse, 49a Goldhawk Road, London W12 8QP

Liolà copyright © 2013 Tanya Ronder

Tanya Ronder has asserted her right to be identified as the author of this version

Cover image: © Corbis and Mary Evans, artwork designed by Matthew Mifsud for original National Theatre production poster © National Theatre
Cover design: Ned Hoste, 2H

Typeset by Nick Hern Books, London
Printed and bound in Great Britain by CPI Group (UK) Ltd

A CIP catalogue record for this book is available from the British Library

ISBN 978 1 84842 343 5

MIX
Paper from responsible sources
FSC® C013604
www.fsc.org

Introduction

Son of Chaos

'A poet of human suffering' is the phrase theatre professor, Ortolani, uses to describe Luigi Pirandello. He urges us to listen for 'the agony echoing from within' the dramas of Italy's enigmatic dramatist. Not a hard ask with most Pirandello plays – they scream misery from the page, tell stories of people trapped in their lives or some nether-life where nobody can exit their vexed reality. Not so, however, with *Liolà*. This is Pirandello on vacation. He wrote it in 1916 after a trip home to Sicily. Pirandello describes this play as a comedy 'full of songs and sunshine… so light-hearted it doesn't seem like one of my works' – and it is uncharacteristically joyful. Yet, light-hearted? He can't shake himself off that easily. The idiosyncratic pain glints brightly beneath the loveliness. Quite apart from the dearth of young men in the world of the play – they emigrated in droves from Sicily in that era to escape poverty and seek work further afield – and the vivid portrait of the limited lot of women, there is the question of what fired Pirandello to write it. Where did the impulse to create the great Sicilian libertine Liolà come from?

Local labourer Liolà is a single father of three boys, each child the offspring of a different woman. Liolà takes full charge of the consequences of his affairs and brings the children up, with his mother's help, uncomplainingly. He works hard, jokes, sings and clearly enjoys sex. A creation of ultimate fecundity, Liolà is at ease with himself and the world around him. Bringing life with him wherever he goes, he is nature's force and has a way with women to make your hair curl. Pirandello, on the other hand, didn't manage women so effortlessly. His marriage slid into extended despair as his wife's nervous disposition escalated into madness, and that was not his only foiled relationship. The lightness in Liolà articulates an absolute counterpoint to the

dogged yearning Pirandello experienced throughout his life. He longed for a fullness of relations with a number of key women, with all of whom it proved impossible. 'I write to forget myself,' he puts in a letter to Marta Abba, the final subject of his unrequited love. Written at the height of Pirandello's difficulties with his wife, Liolà seems to spring out as a form of ideal, the kind of man that Pirandello knew he could never be.

Unsurprisingly, the formative pattern of his parents' relationship was not the healthiest model. His father, Stefano, cheated on Luigi's mother with his niece, no less, with whom he had weekly liaisons in the convent where his sister was prioress. In a short story, Pirandello describes the scene where he, as a youngster, goes and catches them one Sunday. His father hides behind the green curtain, too short to conceal his feet, while the fourteen-year-old Pirandello spits in his unfaithful cousin's face.

Pirandello's first love, at the age of fourteen, was Linuccia, another cousin of his. Four years older than him she was a bright, lovely girl who adored him and may well have been his best chance. By the time he was eighteen, they were engaged, but he was self-conscious doing the mating charade in front of family and community and felt inadequate alongside her several more senior admirers. So he left Sicily and Linuccia, with the engagement still in place. From there on in he was confused about his desires and responsibilities. During this time he had a brief, emancipated liaison whilst studying in Como. He describes the young woman as 'a mistress of vices and an innkeeper of her body' – a blueprint for Liolà, perhaps. They spent every night together, and he believed she was sincere when she swore to be faithful. But it couldn't sustain, and, whichever of them finished it, Luigi moved his studies to Germany, which marked the end of the affair.

In Bonn he met Jenny. She wore a blue mask and straw hat the night they met. He moved to her parents' house as a lodger and befriended the whole family; however, once again a straightforward happiness eluded Pirandello. He was 'a bird without a nest', as he describes himself later in another letter to Marta. He couldn't balance respect for Jenny with sexual intimacy and ended up leaving that transitory roost abruptly and rudely. He returned to Sicily, filled with guilt and feeling like 'a stone', to wriggle out of his engagement with Linuccia, an almost unprecedented move in Sicily at that time.

Perhaps as a consequence of these premature endings, he gave himself completely to the next proposal – his father's suggestion of marrying shy, nunnery-educated Antoinetta Portulano from Agrigento in Sicily. During their courtship, Luigi wrote her tumbling, impassioned letters. 'You are my sun, my peace, my purpose… you will love me, you must love me because I…', he trails off. His outpourings embarrassed and overwhelmed Antoinetta – she didn't know how to respond – but the marriage went ahead, and they had a few timid but content years together in which they produced three children. But after a financial disaster in which Pirandello's father lost all their wealth, Antoinetta had a breakdown. It prompted a lifelong journey into violent paranoia. Everything Luigi did exacerbated her condition. 'It means the failure of any efforts to hide my misery', he wrote of his wife's madness. Luigi chose to care for Antoinetta at home, hoping for her healing and not wanting to give up their conjugal relationship. It was when Antoinetta finally accused Pirandello of having incestuous relations with their sixteen-year-old daughter, Lietta, that Luigi caved in and sent her to a sanatorium where she remained for forty years, well beyond her husband's death. Lietta, traumatised by her mother's behaviour, went away to convent school, Stefano, his oldest son, was a prisoner-of-war in Austria, so Luigi was left acutely lonely with Fausto, his youngest child, in a near-empty house.

A glutton for punishment, he later broke his heart again with an infatuation for the young actress, Marta Abba. Marta became his best friend and muse. She gave him her time, energy and talent, but not her body. They made work together, travelled, toured – he would have followed her in an agony of desire to the ends of the earth. 'I talk to your picture when I am alone,' he confessed to her – just as he also used to converse with his dead mother in the depths of his solitude.

So for Pirandello – for whom the sins of the flesh became and remained a vice – inventing the hero Liolà, whose every encounter is fertile, must have been liberating. He has the attributes more normally found in the protagonist's nemesis, the *competition*. I laughed out loud at Liolà's audacity when I first read the play in the British Library. It's the opposite of *Don Giovanni,* where the rogue male gets his comeuppance and is sent to Hell – this rogue gets no such retribution. Far from it, it is Liolà's new child who will inherit all Uncle Simone's money. With the scattering of his seed, Liolà defies convention, religion and law, yet we inwardly cheer when he persuades Mita to break her marriage vows with him because at base level he is wholesome. He represents the natural forces of the world, the earthly systems rather than our man-made frameworks. He's no 'deviant' but 'pure nature', as he puts it himself. He is rogue in the sense that he is nobody's pet, there's no flock he follows. He has a clear moral viewpoint: it's just not one that society shares.

If it was the foiled longing in Pirandello for what he couldn't enjoy that propelled the transgressive Liolà onto the page, then it is true to the spirit of the 'son of chaos', as Pirandello declared himself. Born in a Sicilian town whose nickname was derived from the Greek *Xaos*, it was a pun, but one with more than an edge of truth. 'With his bones, if not with his head, he knows that life is ironical', says Eric Bentley in his introduction to *Liolà* and four other plays by Pirandello. Liolà's immoral intervention releases such a new burst of life in the villagers and old Simone, and such quiet pleasure in Mita, that we beam, whilst questioning our own dubious moral sense. This schism is the appeal of the play. And although Pirandello may instinctively have felt he'd triumphed in writing a comedy, its shadows are everywhere. Tuzza and Croce are isolated and ruined at the end, and even Liolà, although pleased to have served a good turn, is lonely and aching for a relationship, ideally with Mita though he'd settle for less, which he can never have. A great admirer of *Liolà*, which came early in Pirandello's canon, Bentley also says that the more Pirandello became 'a thinker the less he succeeded in being an artist'.

Richard Eyre knew immediately that he wanted to cast the play with Irish actors for the premiere production at the National Theatre in London. Not to transplant the play to Ireland, but to give us the sound of a forgotten community somewhere on the

West coast while still placing it in rural Sicily. Besides the transferable characteristics – Catholicism (albeit Pirandello's Sicily having a more relaxed form), a tradition of singing, women working, talking, getting by as best they can – the Irishness gave us the earth, heart and tongue which would be all but buried in an English counterpart. Richard was also evangelical about the Taviani Brothers' film, *Kaos*, adapted from several Pirandello short stories. We, especially designer Anthony Ward, took inspiration from this film as a canvas for our Irish actors. *Liolà* feels more tonally linked to *Kaos* than to Pirandello's other plays. It is a stirring film filled with bleak, lingering tenderness yet with bold notes of humour. The camera in *Kaos* gives us access to the characters' unexpressèd feelings. We accentuated these dynamics in *Liolà* by giving voice to some of the women's dejection, both in dialogue and song, so the women's songs aren't confined to work numbers. The music, composed by Orlando Gough, leant towards the Balkan gypsy tradition for its raw soulfulness, and early on in the process we discovered how central the tarantella dance was in Sicily at this time, to help purge women of poison – or in other words, barrenness, sullenness, madness – which the community believed had arisen from the bite of a venomous spider. Scarlett Mackmin worked with the cast to evolve the tarantella in its duality – perfect for the opposing layers in *Liolà* – in its frenzied, trance-like, cathartic form and in its upright celebratory guise.

For all its potential to invite attack of being a misogynist play, in *Liolà* Pirandello gives us a stage full of women with only two central roles for men. And ultimately, to defend Liolà himself, this particular Sicilian is one baby-father who hasn't run off. He's the one bringing up the kids.

Tanya Ronder

English translations by Gaspare Guidice, Susan Bassnett-Mcguire and Benito Ortolani

National Theatre

The National Theatre, where this version of *Liolà* had its premiere in August 2013, is central to the creative life of the UK. In its three theatres on the South Bank in London it presents an eclectic mix of new plays and classics from the world repertoire, with seven or eight productions in repertory at any one time. And through an extensive programme of amplifying activities – Platform performances, backstage tours, foyer music, publications, exhibitions and outdoor events – it recognises that theatre doesn't begin and end with the rise and fall of the curtain. The National endeavours to maintain and re-energise the great traditions of the British stage and to expand the horizons of audiences and artists alike. It aspires to reflect in its repertoire the diversity of the nation's culture. It takes a particular responsibility for the creation of new work – offering at the NT Studio a space for research and development for the NT's stages and the theatre as a whole. Through its Learning programme, it invites people of all ages to discover the NT's repertoire, the skills and excitement of theatre-making, and the building itself. As the national theatre, it aims to foster the health of the wider British theatre through policies of collaboration and touring. These activities demonstrate the considerable public benefit provided by the NT, both locally and nationally. Between twenty and twenty-six new productions are staged each year in one of the NT's three theatres. Last year, the National's total reach was 3.6 million people worldwide, through attendances on the South Bank, in the West End, on tour, and through National Theatre Live, the digital broadcast of live performances to international cinema screens.

Information: +44 (0)20 7452 3400
Box Office: +44 (0)20 7452 3000
National Theatre, South Bank, London SE1 9PX
www.nationaltheatre.org.uk
Registered Charity No: 224223

This version of *Liolà* was first performed in the Lyttelton auditorium of the National Theatre on 7 August 2013 (previews from 31 July). The cast was as follows:

SIMONE PALUMBO	James Hayes
MITA PALUMBO	Lisa Dwyer Hogg
GESA	Rosaleen Linehan
LIOLÀ	Rory Keenan
NINFA	Charlotte Bradley
CÀRMINA	Eileen Walsh
CROCE AZZARA	Aisling O'Sullivan
TUZZA AZZARA	Jessica Regan
NELA	Carla Langley
CIUZZA	Niamh McGowan
LUZZA	Roxanna Nic Liam
TININO	Felix Crutchley *or* Oliver Rosario
CALICCHIO	Tommy Fletcher McMeekin *or* Frederick Neilson
PALLINO	Joseph Stembridge-King *or* Joe Sibley
VILLAGERS	Anthony Delaney
	Jenny Fennessy
	Gertrude Montgomery
	Anne Bird
	David Summer
Director	Richard Eyre
Designer	Anthony Ward
Lighting Designer	Neil Austin
Music	Orlando Gough
Choreographer	Scarlett Mackmin
Sound Designer	Rich Walsh
Literal Translator	Jane Fallowfield

Characters

LIOLÀ, *full name Nico Schillaci, twenty-six*
SIMONE PALUMBO, *landowner, sixty-five*
CROCE AZZARA, *Simone's cousin, fifty*
TUZZA AZZARA, *Croce's daughter, twenty-five*
MITA PALUMBO, *Simone's wife, twenty-four*
CÀRMINA, *nickname La Moscardina (gnat), thirty-eight*
GESA, *Mita's aunt, sixty*
NINFA, *Liolà's mother, fifty-two*
CIUZZA, *sixteen*
LUZZA, *fifteen*
NELA, *fourteen*
TININO, *Liolà's son, five*
CALICCHIO, *Liolà's son, eight*
PALLINO, *Liolà's son, ten*
ANGELO, *violinist, Liolà's friend*
MUSICIANS, *fifties and upwards, male – accordion, guitar,
    double bass, tuba, clarinet, trumpet, percussion*
OTHER VILLAGERS

*A forward slash in the text (/) indicates where the next speaker
starts, overlapping current speech or song.*

*A dash (–) at the end of a speech indicates that the next speaker
cuts in.*

*This text went to press before the end of rehearsals and so may
differ slightly from the play as performed.*

Sicily, June, early 1900s. A MAN *polishes his trumpet in the heat. Other* MUSICIANS *bring their instruments,* VILLAGERS *gather, there is an air of expectation. Two* WOMEN *carry a white sheet, they spread it on the ground in an atmosphere of private ritual. The* MUSICIANS *start to play a tarantella. A young woman in a white nightdress is led to the sheet, this is* MITA. *She lays down. The* WOMEN *gather round, start to sing, stamp, clap and dance to the music, 'na na na na na na na na na na na na na na na'. (Etc.) The volume and speed of the music increases.* MITA *allows it to infect her. First the music's beat can be seen in her body, then the spirit of it infiltrates her. The violinist,* ANGELO, *comes closer, plays just for* MITA. MITA *writhes, shakes and thrusts, goaded by a stern-looking* SIMONE. *It becomes an exorcism, as if she were expelling poison. She grabs at a red scarf, embroils it in her thrashings.* MITA's *energy is roused to its highest as the music reaches a crescendo. She grows limp, exhausted. The music drops, everything is quiet. A little shaky,* MITA *stands up, speaks to us.*

MITA. I'm Mita, an orphan.

SIMONE *introduces himself to us.*

SIMONE. Simone, landowner.

MITA. I married him. We've no children.

SIMONE. Yet.

It's noon, the sun is high. MITA *is handed a large stone and a small rock, she sits. One of a number of baskets is placed near her, it is full of almonds. She starts to shell the nuts, smashing the rock down on her anchor stone, it's hard, concentrated work.* GESA *brings a chair forward.*

GESA. I'm Gesa, Mita's aunt, but she's a daughter to me. My sons are long gone, America, Milan.

She joins the shelling. NINFA *comes forward with*
PALLINO, TININO *and* CALICCHIO.

NINFA. I'm Ninfa, her neighbour.

She and GESA *acknowledge one another. She indicates*
PALLINO, CALICCHIO *and* TININO.

These three, my grandchildren. I'm trying to get to Mass.

As she and the BOYS *leave, the church bell sounds.*
CÀRMINA *steps forward with a chair.*

CÀRMINA. I'm Càrmina, neither wife nor mother nor nothing,
but I sing.

CROCE *hands her a stone and rock.*

CROCE. And I'm Croce Azzara, their boss this Sunday. Cousin
to the real boss.

She indicates SIMONE. *The* WOMEN*'s pounding provides
an off-beat to the church bells, 'smash, dang, smash, dang,
smash, dang'. They sing as they work, lifting off from the*
MUSICIANS. *It's muted, just for themselves.*

CÀRMINA (*singing*).
　　Dragged along the stony path
　　Silent as a tomb,
　　Pilate follows with a staff,
　　Wicked from the womb.

LUZZA, CIUZZA *and* NELA *come and sit with* MITA.
They speak over the chorus.

WOMEN (*singing*).
　　/ Ha la ya la ya la ya la la
　　Ha la ya la ya la ya la la
　　Wicked from the womb.

NELA. I'm Nela.

CIUZZA. I'm Ciuzza.

LUZZA. And I'm Luzza.

They join the shelling.

CÀRMINA (*singing*).
> 'Guards,' he says
> 'Take off his clothes,
> Crown him with these thorns,
> Make sure everybody knows
> He will be dead by dawn!'

TUZZA *walks down, glowers at us, speaks over the chorus.*

WOMEN (*singing*).
> / Ha la ya la ya la ya la la
> Ha la ya la ya la ya la la
> Will be dead by dawn.

TUZZA. I'm Tuzza. I've got no brothers and a dead father, but I'm her daughter – (CROCE.) so also his cousin.

She points at SIMONE, *who is monitoring the shelling. She sits with the older* WOMEN.

WOMEN (*singing*).
> Our Holy Father's only son
> Looks up at us and smiles.
> His torment only just begun
> His holy form defiled.

LIOLÀ *steps forward, speaks to us over the chorus.*

> / Ha la ya la ya la ya la la
> Ha la ya la ya la ya la la
> Ha la ya la ya la ya la la
> Ha la ya la ya la ya la la
> Ha la ya la ya la ya la la
> Ha la ya la ya la ya la la
> Ha la ya la ya la ya la la
> Ha la ya la ya la ya la la
> His holy form defiled.

LIOLÀ. Though he might surprise himself, when a man wants a wife he dresses in the best he can muster. Not much. A clean shirt, a hat.

He acknowledges ANGELO, *the violinist, as he pinches his hat.*

Angelo.

Back to us.

And boots. Found one night discarded, like a miracle, as I escaped barefoot across a wall.

Beat.

I'm Liolà, by the way.

He goes.

WOMEN (*singing*).
> Mary hides behind the door
> As he receives his whipping…

CROCE *brings more nuts.*

CÀRMINA (*singing*).
> 'Please don't give him any more,
> His wounds are dripping.'

CROCE. Here's the last, then, God willing, we'll have shelled our fill.

The conversation continues as the WOMEN *sing.*

WOMEN (*singing*).
> / Ha la ya la ya la ya la la
> Ha la ya la ya la ya la la
> Ha la ya la ya la ya la la
> Ha la ya la ya la ya la la… (*Etc.*)
> His wounds are dripping.

CÀRMINA. Not for long.

LUZZA. 'Til September, just.

NELA. When the next harvest's in.

GESA. And it all begins again. A brief holiday from a year of cracking nuts.

CIUZZA. I can take more.

LUZZA. And me.

NELA. And me.

Distributing the nuts.

CROCE. Pace it up, girls, you might make it for Mass.

NELA. Next week's?

LUZZA. We have to go home first.

NELA. Get changed.

GESA. Because you have to look your best for Jesus, right, girls?

NELA. You want us sitting in church like pigs?

CIUZZA. I'm going like this.

NELA. Are you?

CROCE. If you don't stop chattering, you'll be listening through the door.

CÀRMINA. A good thing too, if you're not changing, Ciuzza.

It's good-humoured banter. LUZZA *reaches over, tries to smell* CIUZZA.

CIUZZA. Get off!

SIMONE (*to* LUZZA). Stop wasting time, you little shrimp.

LUZZA. Come on, Càrmina, let's sing.

SIMONE. No, you don't...

They fall back to hammering and singing with renewed gusto.

CÀRMINA (*singing*).
   'Take me to him, lead me, lead.'

WOMEN (*singing*).
   / 'Dear, you cannot walk.'

SIMONE (*over the song*). All morning the Passion and it's the middle of June!

CÀRMINA (*singing*).
  'I must be near him, let me see.'

WOMEN (*singing*).
  / 'It will make your soul distraught.'

  SIMONE *shouts over them.*

SIMONE. Stop, stop, stop, that's enough, you are splitting my head!

  Reluctantly, they stop singing and return to cracking in silence.

NELA. What a grouch.

SIMONE. I can't say what's worse, shelling or singing.

LUZZA. You can't do one without the other.

CIUZZA. You don't have to be here, Uncle Simone.

GESA. Your headache's your bad conscience, Uncle, making us work Sunday.

SIMONE. What do you mean, me? Mother Croce engaged you.

CROCE. Cousin, are you blaming me?

SIMONE. It is you.

CROCE. The days you bullied me for. 'We have to shift them, the new season will be on us...'

  (*To the* WOMEN.) You should have heard the tales of misery if we didn't shell today – bankruptcy, poverty...

SIMONE (*ironic*). Because they're such a mine of wealth for me.

CÀRMINA. You're not backing out of that drink you promised are you, Uncle?

CROCE. It's not a promise, it's part of the deal.

SIMONE. For a handful of cracked nuts, are you serious?

CROCE. You can't change your mind now, cousin.

(*To* MITA.) Run up to the house, Mita, fetch a jug-full, we'll drink to your husband's health and wealth.

NELA. Yes, go on, Mita.

LUZZA. Quick!

NELA. Bring two jugs!

CIUZZA. Do you want me to come with you?

CROCE. You've worked hard, and it is Sunday.

MITA *doesn't move. The church bells stop.*

CÀRMINA. Well, Mita?

CROCE. Why aren't you going?

MITA. He hasn't asked me to.

CROCE. Is it not your wine as well?

MITA. No.

Pause. The WOMEN *look between* MITA *and* SIMONE.

SIMONE. Cousin, if I am tempted again another year to purchase your almonds before they're harvested, see these eyes? (*His own.*) I will pluck them out.

CROCE. Come, now, cousin. The coming harvest will be healthier, I'm sure.

LUZZA. It's what almonds are like.

NELA. Stacks one year, none the next.

SIMONE. If the almonds were all. Take a walk round my vineyards. And my olives, the tops of my olive trees are withering already, it's not even July.

CÀRMINA. Listen to you whine, you're a rich man, Uncle. You guessed a tree's crop, it fell short. At least your loss is your cousin's gain. (*Pointedly.*) Your widowed cousin and her fatherless daughter.

CIUZZA. Any money you paid stays in the family.

LUZZA. Would you rather keep it to be buried with you when you die?

CÀRMINA. Because with no children to inherit –

She stops abruptly.

Sorry. Sorry, Mita, it just slipped out.

SIMONE *glares at* CÀRMINA.

SIMONE (*to* MITA). Go home. Go on, get out of my sight, you deadweight.

MITA *stands.*

See what your uselessness brings? You turn me into a man they humiliate. Go, or, by God I can't vouch for what I might do this morning.

MITA *leaves, mortified.* SIMONE *kicks something and leaves.*

CROCE. Holy Father, Càrmina, your tongue!

CÀRMINA. It just slipped out. He was asking for it.

CROCE. You're a wasp.

CIUZZA (*ingenuous*). Is he so ashamed of having no children?

CROCE. Hush, Ciuzza, you're too young to understand.

LUZZA. No she's not, she's sixteen!

NELA. What's hard to understand? God's not given him babies.

LUZZA. But why does he blame his wife?

CROCE. Will you stop philosophising and sort the nuts.

CIUZZA. We're going to Mass.

CROCE. So, leave.

The GIRLS move off, but not far.

LUZZA. Hey, Tuzza.

NELA. What's wrong?

TUZZA. Go away.

The WOMEN *close in for a quiet bitch while they sort the nuts from the shells. The* GIRLS *take it in turns to come close enough to hear.*

CROCE. Dear God, Uncle Simone never lets up. He's been bloating my head with his woes all week.

CÀRMINA. What does he expect you to do, give him a child yourself?

CROCE. He wants one that much, I would if I could.

CÀRMINA. If whinging was all you needed to give life.

GESA. He'd have schoolrooms full by now.

CROCE. The thing that really upsets him is, who'll get the money? Imagining what'll happen to all his furniture, the house, that's what clutches his soul.

CÀRMINA. Enjoy his woe, Mother Croce, so long as he's childless, you're laughing.

CROCE. The man has more relatives than nuts.

CÀRMINA. But still, as a close relation, you'll get a good share. It's poor Mita who should worry, the way he is with her. And where there are no children, all the husband's possessions –

GESA (*jumping in*). Get shoved down his gullet along with the Devil.

CROCE. Gesa.

GESA. And he can choke on the lot because it's killing my Mita. You'd think she were a floor, the way he tramples on her. I'm the one who brought her up – only God knows how at times – but what can I do? Her mother dies when she's in the crib, her father gets kicked in the head by his horse… if she had a father or a brother now, he wouldn't dare treat her that way.

CÀRMINA. Everyone thought she was the luckiest girl in the world, picked to marry Simone Palumbo. I know I did.

GESA. Ha!

CÀRMINA. Well. Cherries and plums are pleasant, but not if you have no bread.

CROCE. Oh wait, you're not telling me that marriage hasn't been lucky for Mita? Come on. I mean, she's a good girl, I'm not saying she's not, but Mita couldn't have dreamed of becoming the wife of my cousin, he's the richest man for miles!

CÀRMINA (*deadpan*). The only man for miles.

GESA. Who begged your cousin to take her, Croce – me? No. Mita? No.

CROCE. I can't believe what you're saying. You saw his first wife, Donna Madalena – she was a proper lady!

CÀRMINA. He wept buckets when she died.

GESA. For the sons she'd not given him. Where were Donna Madalena's pregnancies? Conspicuous by their absence, no?

CROCE. She was never going to get pregnant, she was a sickly thing, a stick.

(*Indicates with her finger.*) Always teetering on the edge of life.

CÀRMINA. But he loved her.

GESA. He loved the good life, her fancy tastes.

CROCE. What I'm saying is when she died, he was not without options.

CÀRMINA. No.

CROCE. Take my daughter, for example, if he'd wanted to marry Tuzza, I'd have given her to him, no question. But he didn't want a relative, none of his relatives and all of them tried, especially not a close cousin like Tuzza. So he chose Mita, for the children she would bear him.

The three GIRLS *are giggling, running to and from the gossip.*

GESA. Forgive me, Mother Croce, but are you blaming Mita for not falling pregnant?

CROCE *gets surprised by* LUZZA.

CROCE. Shit, you little snitch, I told you, get out of here!

(*To* CÀRMINA *and* GESA.) Sorry.

CÀRMINA. Gorgeous, comely Mita? She's the picture of health.

GESA. A rose.

CROCE. That needn't mean anything. Oftentime –

CÀRMINA (*interrupting her*). You said it yourself.

Repeating CROCE*'s stick-motion with her finger.*

That wasn't going to be fruitful, was it?

GESA. Come on, Croce, set Mita and Simone side by side, anyone can see which of them's lacking.

CROCE. He wouldn't go around shouting about having children if he couldn't have any, would he?

CÀRMINA. Wouldn't he?

GESA. He should be thankful my niece is such an honest girl. Whether he's up to the task or not will never be proven, though a saint would be pushed being treated that way. The Virgin Mary herself would shout, 'You want a child? Wait there, I'll go and make one for you.'

Beat.

CÀRMINA. Mita would never do such a thing.

GESA. God in Heaven, she wouldn't.

CÀRMINA. A mortal sin, it would be.

GESA. And doesn't she know it. She'd sooner be struck by lightning than go behind his back.

CÀRMINA. Mita's always been that way, pure-hearted from when she was tiny. I don't mean disrespect to the other girls, but she's a special one, your niece.

TUZZA is listening, unimpressed.

CROCE. I don't deny it, Mita is a good girl.

CIUZZA. Look, it's Liolà's chicks!

From the back, the BOYS appear. The GIRLS call them over.

Tinino.

LUZZA. Calicchio.

NELA. Pallino.

The BOYS run to the GIRLS. NINFA comes after them.

CIUZZA. Who's my boy?

TININO. Me.

LUZZA (*to* CALICCHIO). Who's mine?

CALICCHIO. I am.

NELA. What about you, Pallino, whose are you?

PALLINO. Uh, yours.

The BOYS nuzzle into the GIRLS, letting themselves be hugged and kissed.

CÀRMINA. Look at that, the wolf's babies born with teeth.

NINFA. For heaven's sake, girls, put the boys down, don't distract them, look what time I'm heading to Mass... what a morning.

GESA. I'm glad I only had one child dumped on me.

NINFA. Ah, they're good lads.

CROCE. Without a mother to rub together.

CÀRMINA (*to* NINFA). You're lucky it's just three of them, the way your son is with girls.

CROCE (*indicating the* BOYS). Steady, Càrmina…

CÀRMINA. I'm not saying he's not a good dad, he always has been, even as a teenager. Who else would be happy to bring up the offspring from those kinds of women?

NINFA. He wants more children, dreams of a whole choir of them.

For the BOYS' *benefit*.

Then he'll put them in a big cage and take them up to the town to sell.

CIUZZA. Shall we put you in a cage, Tinino, like a goldfinch? Sing something.

TININO *runs off*.

TININO. No!

CÀRMINA (*indicating* PALLINO). Is this one Rosa la Favarese's?

NINFA. Pallino? Do you know, I don't remember, was Rosa first? No, I think Calicchio is Rosa's son, isn't he?

CIUZZA (*grabbing him*). Tinino's mine!

GESA. You'd be in trouble if that were so, Ciuzza.

NINFA (*to* GESA). I take offence at that, neighbour.

GESA. I didn't mean…

CÀRMINA. Come on, Mother Ninfa, she's sixteen.

NINFA. Liolà was a father at sixteen.

CROCE. Another few months and she'll be ripe pickings.

CÀRMINA. You can't honestly say it would be a good thing to be Liolà's wife?

NINFA. My son is the most loving and respectful boy on earth.

CÀRMINA. Loving, I'll grant you, he sees a hundred, he wants a hundred.

NINFA. That's just because he's not found his one.

She looks at TUZZA.

Right, I'm on my way, girls. What's the matter, Tuzza, you don't look well?

TUZZA (*graceless*). Nothing.

CÀRMINA. A case of the sulks.

CROCE. She was feverish last night.

GESA. I'll go too, Mother Croce, if we're done?

CÀRMINA. Are you not waiting for your drink, Gesa?

GESA. You'll be lucky.

The church bells stop again.

That's afternoon Mass starting.

CIUZZA. Ah, well.

NINFA. This time last week when all the smart ladies oozed in, leaving their kitchens to other cooks, I tell you I couldn't concentrate on Mass at all.

CIUZZA. Why, what were they doing?

NINFA. The Devil slipped behind my eyes, all I could see was their fans.

LUZZA. What do you mean?

NINFA. Look, ladies, and learn.

She improvises a fan.

The ones who are not yet married...

She lifts her chest and shakes her fan heavily and rapidly.

'He's going to be mine, he's going to be mine, he's going to be mine.' The married ones...

She moves her hand with calm, satisfied strokes.

'He's mine, mine, all mine.' Then the widows, poor loves...

Her fan-hand slumps down.

'Was he mine... or am I dreaming?'

Everyone laughs.

I kept crossing myself to distract me, but I was hypnotised.

The GIRLS create fans of their own.

CIUZZA, LUZZA *and* NELA. Oh, yes! – He's going to be mine, he's going to be mine, he's going to be mine, he's going to be mine.

CÀRMINA. That's the peak of their day.

Open-throated, playful singing.

LIOLÀ (*singing, off*).
    It's so many days since I saw you
    I've been chained like a dog,
    Chained like a dog,
    Kept from Heaven's due.

LIOLÀ *appears, putting on a jacket to complete his outfit.*

    Your opal eyes and velvet skin,
    Opal eyes and velvet skin,
    New life, they whisper, will begin,
    New life, they whisper, will begin.

The MUSICIANS accompany him.

CIUZZA, LUZZA *and* NELA. Liolà!

CALICCHIO, PALLINO *and* TININO. Papa!

NINFA. I'll never get to Mass now.

LIOLÀ. You've found your mothers, have you, boys?

The GIRLS laugh, abashed. He swings each BOY up.

My star – (TININO.) my sun – (CALICCHIO.) my moon – (PALLINO.)

(*To* NINFA.) How come you're here, I thought you were at church?

NINFA. No, look, I'm going, I'm going...

LIOLÀ. You can't trek up there now, it's started, you'll be stood out on the cobbles.

NINFA. I should still go.

CÀRMINA. To gawp at the ladies.

LIOLÀ. Forget it, Mother. God be with you, Mother Croce.

CROCE. And you. Just hold your distance, young man.

Beat.

LIOLÀ. And what if I didn't want to?

CROCE. I'd get the rolling pin out and bash you over the head.

CIUZZA. Spill some of his wild blood.

LIOLÀ (*to* CIUZZA). You'd like that, would you, to see some blood from inside my head?

He grabs her and tickles her. The three GIRLS *scream, good-humouredly.* LUZZA *and* NELA *come to* CIUZZA*'s rescue.*

LUZZA. Get off, maniac!

CIUZZA. Get your hands off me!

NELA. Get off her!

CROCE. They're barely children, these girls.

LIOLÀ. Of course they're children, look at them. Don't go rushing anyone from childhood, Mother Croce.

The GIRLS *are giggling and rosy-cheeked.*

CÀRMINA. What's the outfit in aid of, Liolà?

NELA. Tell us!

LUZZA. It's for me, isn't it?

He struts around, showing off his clothes.

LIOLÀ. Am I handsome? It's important you say 'yes', because I'm getting married.

CIUZZA. Married? Which devil are you marrying?

LIOLÀ. You, my deviless, don't you want me?

CIUZZA. I'd rather marry your horse!

LIOLÀ. You then, Luzza, what do you say?

LUZZA. I wouldn't want you.

LIOLÀ. Oh, wouldn't you?

LUZZA. No.

LIOLÀ. You can be high and mighty because you know I'd have none of you. One breath and you'd come flying, but what would I do with butterflies like you?

> (*Singing.*)
> My queen will own me body and soul,
> Girl of beauty, heart of gold,
> For her I'll do just what I'm told
> For her alone, no other.

CIUZZA, LUZZA *and* NELA. More, Liolà! – Sing another one! – More! (*Etc.*)

Talking about the songs:

GESA. He unfolds them like vapour.

NINFA. Easy as turning a rosary.

CÀRMINA. Go on, Liolà, don't make us beg.

CIUZZA, LUZZA *and* NELA. Liolà, Liolà, Liolà.

LIOLÀ. Who ever never needed begging?

Again, the band of MUSICIANS *support his song.*

(*To his* BOYS.) This one's for you three.

> (*Singing.*)
> See me, boys,
> Come close,
> Closer,
> My arms are steady

But inside my mind,
It reels.
Feel
The wind
Rush by
It turns me
Spins my ground
Turns me
Turns
Turns
Turns
Aaeee…

He spins and stamps, the BOYS *spin, everyone stamps and claps to gee them on.*

Here today I burn for you,
For every perfect thing you do
To me.
Tomorrow, sweet,
The wind has blown
You'll learn my heart
Was never
Yours
To own.
See the spark
Dance the breeze
It's me
It's me
It's me
It's gone.
So long.

CÀRMINA. This is how you'll find your queen, is it, by promising your disappearance?

LIOLÀ. It's a song, Càrmina. And how do you know I've not found her already?

CÀRMINA. Ha.

LIOLÀ. Why d'you laugh? Those who can't keep a secret will never be king.

CROCE (*stopping the* BOYS *from making mess*). That's enough now, boys, come on.

CÀRMINA. What's happened to our wine?

CROCE. After your indiscretion?

CÀRMINA. That's a broken deal! Do you know why Uncle Simone won't give us a drink, Liolà?

LIOLÀ. No.

CÀRMINA. Because I said he didn't have any children.

LIOLÀ. He doesn't.

CIUZZA. Exactly.

LIOLÀ. Is that why Mita's not here?

GESA. He sent her home.

LIOLÀ. Did he? Where is he?

CÀRMINA. He's in there.

CÀRMINA *points.* LIOLÀ *calls to him.*

LIOLÀ. Simone, Uncle Simone, would you mind coming out the storehouse a minute, I have some news.

SIMONE *emerges from the back.*

SIMONE. Can't be good news, if you're the messenger.

LIOLÀ. It's exceptional news. They've invented a law to improve our lives.

SIMONE. Oh, right.

LIOLÀ. You want to hear it?

SIMONE. Go on then.

LIOLÀ. The man with a sow who births twenty piglets is rich, isn't he? When he sells. The more piglets she has, the richer he is. Same with a cow – the more calves, the wealthier the farmer, you know?

SIMONE. Yes.

LIOLÀ. Consider then, a poor fellow with these women of ours. As soon as you so much as touch them their bellies swell, you know? So, as an answer of sorts, our thoughtful government has brought back an ancient law. All Sicilians are now allowed to sell sons. We can buy and sell children, Uncle Simone, and look, look what I have three of.

Displaying his sons.

I could open a shop! Who'd like a boy, this one here? A lovely piece of meat, feel him, firm, juicy, weighs around twenty kilos. Do you know how much I'm asking? To you? Nothing. Not a thing, except a barrel of your cherry wine.

The WOMEN *laugh.*

SIMONE. Don't play with me, Liolà.

LIOLÀ. If you want one, buy one.

SIMONE. Take your hands off me!

LIOLÀ. Calm down, Simone, you're behaving like a cockerel fresh from the chop.

SIMONE. Get out of my sight, you waster, you oaf, or you won't know what's hit you!

LIOLÀ. Oh, come now, Uncle, don't take offence, we're neighbours, we're *all* a bunch of oafs. One good deed deserves another, that's all. I'm productive, you're not...

SIMONE. Who says I'm not productive?

CÀRMINA. You show him, Uncle.

LIOLÀ (*to* SIMONE). I'd love to see that miracle, with this one, maybe, or this? Look, that one's sweet.

He offers the three GIRLS *up in turn.*

CROCE. All right, game over...

LIOLÀ. They're children, Croce, they can take a joke.

All three GIRLS *find it very funny.*

CROCE (*to* SIMONE). Are you all right, cousin?

CÀRMINA. A drink might set him straight.

LIOLÀ. It's pure mathematics. I have lots of sons with nothing to inherit, Uncle Simone has no sons with lots to inherit. My flesh is still springy whereas his has lost its elasticity. Try – poke him and the mark will stay on his skin for days.

SIMONE. I'll leave my damned mark on you!

SIMONE *goes for* LIOLÀ *but overbalances.*

LIOLÀ. It's not a judgement, Uncle Simone, just fact. You should try ironised wine.

CIUZZA. What's that?

LUZZA. What is it?

NELA. What's ironised wine?

LIOLÀ. Take a red hot poker, plunge it in to dark wine, let it cool, then drink a long, deep draft. It works wonders.

CIUZZA. Really?

LIOLÀ. You're lucky they've not taken your land away, yet.

SIMONE. Whose, mine?

LIOLÀ. A law could be passed at any moment. Look.

He demonstrates.

Here's a piece of earth. If you stand guard over it, watching it, waiting, what happens? Nothing. Apply those same rules to women? No babies.

SIMONE. The bare-faced cheek –

LIOLÀ. Hear me out, Uncle. So, you have your prized piece of earth, then you get me along to hoe it, fertilise it for you. I dig a hole, throw in some seed, lo and behold, a sapling springs up – but who does the tree belong to? Which of us did the earth give it to? You claim it as yours, Uncle, because your foot is on the land, but does the land know who owns her? The ground offers its fruit to whoever farms it. Right now, you get the pickings because that's what the law says, but tomorrow or the next day the law could turn in favour of the farmhands. You should be prepared because, when it does, you'll be shoved off and you won't be able to take the land with you.

SIMONE. You're devious and scheming...

LIOLÀ. I'm no deviant, pure nature, me, and I want nothing from you. I'll leave you to beat your own brains up about your riches. (*To* CROCE.) What's to be done, Aunt, these almonds up to Uncle's store?

CROCE. Yes, Liolà.

LIOLÀ. Come on then, girls. And just perhaps, Uncle Simone will give us a drink up at the house.

(*Singing.*)
     I slept last night the sleep I love,
     The velvet sky, the stars above,
     My bed a simple patch of earth...

(*Handing* NELA *a basket.*) You got it, Nela?

NELA. Yep.

LIOLÀ. Luzza.

He gives her a basket.

Ciuzza!

Another basket.

(*Singing.*)
     Hunger, worry, thirst and fear,
     Don't fool me, don't spill tears,
     Why cry
     When you can sing instead?

Come on, Càrmina, don't skulk. A small one for you, Aunt Gesa. That's it, that's the lot, let's go!

He takes the biggest basket by far. They set off with their loads, the others picking up more of the tune.

LIOLÀ *and* OTHERS (*singing*).
>For all, I wish the sun and health,
>To me, a lovely girl is wealth,
>And all those curly babies' heads.
>My mother is as fine as sun
>I wish her like on everyone
>Our house is filled with beds.

He has an affectionate moment with his mother. SIMONE *goes with them, carrying nothing.*

SIMONE (*to* CROCE). I'll return with the money, cousin.

CROCE. Whenever's convenient, cousin.

LIOLÀ. Come on, boys, keep up, we'll sell one of you eventually.

He turns back to CROCE.

I'll be back, too, Aunt Croce, I need to speak with you.

CROCE. With me?

TUZZA *jumps to her feet.*

LIOLÀ. What's up with you?

CROCE. What is up with you?

LIOLÀ (*kindly*). Stomach ache, probably.

CROCE. What would you know?

LIOLÀ. Not much, Aunt Croce. See you soon.

LIOLÀ *goes, joining the singing again.*

>For all, I wish the sun and health,
>To me, a lovely girl is wealth,
>And all those curly babies' heads. (*Etc.*)

They head off. CROCE *looks at her daughter.* ANGELO *continues playing the violin, quietly.*

TUZZA. Don't look at me, I don't want him. I don't want him, I don't want him!

Beat.

CROCE. What are you saying, Tuzza?

TUZZA. He's going to come back and ask you for my hand so I'm telling you now, I don't want him.

CROCE. How would he dare to ask for your hand in marriage?

TUZZA. I don't want him, Mother, believe me.

CROCE. I need a straight answer, my girl, have you been with him?

She looks TUZZA *in the eyes.* CROCE *is horrified.*

Oh my God. When, where? Answer me!

TUZZA (*quietly*). Don't shout, everybody will hear.

ANGELO*'s playing ups in tempo. It seems to needle the argument to life.*

CROCE. You stupid, mindless, filth. Are you pregnant? Is that what he meant by 'stomach ache'? Holy Mother of God, you are going to tell me every last thing!

The village swells to its capacity as the VILLAGERS *are drawn back in to surround* CROCE *and* TUZZA. CROCE *attacks* TUZZA.

TUZZA. No, Mother, don't…

CROCE. Speak to me, you worthless girl.

The tune turns wild and mournful with an edgy gypsy energy. We can hardly see TUZZA *and* CROCE *amid the* VILLAGERS, *just hear their shouts.*

TUZZA. Stop it, stop it.

CROCE. I should never have let you out of my sight! I should have guessed you'd be so stupid. Where's my wooden spoon!

TUZZA. Leave me alone!

CROCE. Tell me now, how many times? Where did you take him? I can't hear you!

TUZZA. You told me Uncle would pick me, that's what you said to me, I'd marry Uncle Simone!

CROCE. Are you retarded?

The music finally subdues, the VILLAGERS *recede,* CROCE *emerges, very ruffled. Then she holds* TUZZA *to her.*

I'll kill you dead, I'll kill you dead, on Sunday, of all days. Stay my hand, Lord, or I will finish her off. The gall to tell me it's my fault, me, who put the thought of marrying Simone into your head.

Her fury escalates again.

So you go and do it with that lawless lowlife?

TUZZA, *battered and dishevelled, squares up to her mother.*

TUZZA. Yes, Mother, that is what I did.

CROCE. You need to get out of my sight, Tuzza, or, as God is my witness –

TUZZA. Do you want to hear me speak, or not?

CROCE. Look at your brazen face, hear you speak?

TUZZA. First, it's, slap, punch, kick, 'speak!', but now that I have something to say…

CROCE. What could you possibly say that's of any value?

TUZZA. I want to tell you why I went with Liolà.

CROCE. I know why you went with him, you little hussy, I should tether you like a billy goat!

TUZZA. It was because of Mita.

CROCE. Mita?

TUZZA. When Uncle Simone chose little saint Mita over me, I knew she still had eyes for Liolà.

CROCE. So? She marries Simone, end of the matter.

TUZZA. Not end of the matter. Liolà circles Mita like a moth to a flame, and she's no different.

CROCE. They were brought up together, next-door neighbours.

TUZZA. Five years and nothing's changed. I decided to take him from her.

CROCE. Is that so?

TUZZA. How many things does one annoying orphan girl need? The richest of all the husbands and Liolà, the lover, forever hers.

CROCE. And you call her stupid. The only one you've damaged here, Tuzza, is your brainless self, and the only option you have left is to marry Liolà.

TUZZA. A man who's given himself away a thousand times and who still loves Mita, are you joking?

CROCE. God give me strength.

TUZZA. I'm happier lost, and I would tell you why if you'd only listen.

CROCE. Educate me.

TUZZA. Because she'll be lost too. She was the cause, she'll bear the brunt.

CROCE (*talking about* TUZZA). Dear God, she's losing her mind.

TUZZA. I'm not. Yesterday, Uncle Simone... (*Stops.*)

CROCE. What has he got to do with this?

TUZZA. It wasn't the first time he said he regretted marrying Mita instead of me.

CROCE. Tuzza, you haven't... have you?

TUZZA. With Uncle Simone? No!

CROCE. What are you playing at, then?

TUZZA. How many relatives does Uncle have?

CROCE. Dozens.

TUZZA. How many children?

CROCE. None.

TUZZA. I couldn't do anything about it, before now.

CROCE. You want Uncle Simone to think that your child is his?

TUZZA. How could I make him think that when I've not been with him? You ask such stupid questions. No, I'll throw myself at his feet and beg his protection.

CROCE. Then?

TUZZA. Then, he will have a baby. We'll make out to everybody else, especially his wife, that the child is his. He'll be so happy to have a baby, he won't care how it's come about.

TUZZA smooths her hair.

CROCE. You're a devil, you are, a devil's child.

TUZZA. I'm your child.

CROCE. You want everyone to think...?

TUZZA. Why not, I'm already sunk.

CROCE. He's here, returning with Liolà, get inside.

TUZZA goes straight away. CROCE mutters to herself.

Mother of God, what am I to say? I can't do this.

She picks up a broom and, trying to look cheerful, sweeps up the remaining shells. LIOLÀ comes forward with SIMONE.

LIOLÀ (*to* SIMONE). Hand over the money, Uncle, then if you don't mind, leave us. Mother Croce and I have things to discuss.

CROCE. Who are you to speak to him that way? I'll have you know, this is a second home to my cousin. Go in, Simone, please, go on in, Tuzza's inside.

SIMONE. I only came to settle up...

CROCE. Oh, if you wish, or it can wait, you're the boss, but do step inside. (*Calling.*) Tuzza, your uncle's here. (*To* SIMONE.) And I'll listen to what this madman has to say.

SIMONE. Guard your ears, his foolish tongue makes you cross-eyed.

SIMONE *goes to join* TUZZA. LIOLÀ *and* CROCE *are alone. There's a silence.*

LIOLÀ. Ah, right.

CROCE. What?

LIOLÀ. Nothing. I did want to have a talk, but… I think I'm too late. There was I offering to sell a son, but actually he wants one for free.

CROCE. You're raving.

LIOLÀ. I saw how Tuzza jumped when I said I wanted to talk. Her hair stood on end like a palm tree.

CROCE. She doesn't like you.

LIOLÀ. Then you wheedle your cousin into the house with that soapy, slippery manner.

CROCE. Do you have special dispensation, Liolà, to give orders as to who comes and goes in our house?

LIOLÀ. I've come here to do my duty, Mother Croce.

CROCE. What duty might that be?

LIOLÀ. You know I'm a bird on the wing, here today, elsewhere tomorrow. Replete with sunshine and music, that's who I am. That said, I'm here with a pair of clippers offering to cut my wings, step into a cage of my own making. I've come to ask you for your daughter's hand in marriage, Mother Croce.

CROCE. Are you joking? Are you asking me to give Tuzza, my only child, to a man like you?

LIOLÀ. Thank you for your honesty, Mother, you've swung my cage door wide. Yet, I can't walk away without telling you, you must give Tuzza to me, not for my sake, but for hers.

CROCE. My beautiful daughter? Liolà, I'd see her hanged rather than marry you. You've ruined three girls already and now you come offering yourself here.

LIOLÀ. I've ruined no one and you know it.

CROCE. Did you birth your sons yourself? You're like those snakes who wrap themselves round the cows' ankles and suckle all the milk.

LIOLÀ. You know who birthed them. Of course it's wrong to force a well-guarded gate, but a boy who follows an open path, well. The kind of beaten road I met those girls on was full of travellers who wouldn't hesitate to break down a door, but that's not my way. And how could I regret my sons? They keep my mother busy, they'll help me as they grow older. I'm not a bad provider, Mother Croce – stableman, day-labourer, farmhand, I mow, prune, plant, cut the hay... Like your oven at Easter, I go on for ever.

CROCE. Have you finished preaching, because it won't wash with me.

LIOLÀ. Don't give me this, Mother, I came here with an honest heart. I don't want to disgrace anyone. But nor should anyone use me to create disgrace. If Tuzza refuses me, I'd like to hear that from her, in the presence of Uncle Simone.

CROCE. She doesn't want you, is that clear? She told me so just now, again and again.

LIOLÀ. Did she now?

Beat. He makes a bolt towards TUZZA, CROCE *stops him. They have a stand-off.*

Mother Croce!

CROCE. Liolà!

LIOLÀ. I want to hear Tuzza say it, in front of Uncle Simone.

CROCE. Do you never give up? She doesn't want to see you, she doesn't want to speak to you, go away. It's better for you that way, anyhow.

LIOLÀ. It's not better for somebody else though, is it?

CROCE. I don't know what you're talking about.

LIOLÀ. You won't manage it, Mother Croce.

He proffers his arm.

Smell this.

CROCE. What are you doing? Get off.

LIOLÀ. Can you smell?

CROCE. Rotten meat.

LIOLÀ. It's the scent of fair play. I don't lose a game from underhand shuffling. I hold the cards in my head like words to a song, remember that, Mother. For now, I'll lay my hand down and say so long.

CROCE. Go away and stay away, far, far away.

The afternoon's drawing in. LIOLÀ *loiters near where* TUZZA *is and sings, gently underscored by the* MUSICIANS.

LIOLÀ (*singing*).
>	My girl, she thinks she is a winner,
>	She leaps, she dares
>	You take the chance, you risk the fall,
>	Left holding thin air…

(*Speaking.*) 'Til next time, Mother Croce.

He goes, humming and singing. CROCE *paces, anxious.* SIMONE *and* TUZZA *come forward.* TUZZA *is exhausted with crying,* SIMONE *is flustered.* CROCE *shushes them until* LIOLÀ *is beyond earshot.*

SIMONE. What did that vagabond want?

LIOLÀ (*singing, off*).
>	Left holding thin air…

SIMONE *suddenly realises.*

SIMONE. It's his child. That's what he was doing here.

TUZZA *hides her face in shame.*

Does Liolà know?

TUZZA. That I'm pregnant?

CROCE. No.

TUZZA. No, nobody knows.

SIMONE. I'm glad.

(*To* CROCE.) On this promise, cousin. That nobody will ever know, and that the baby... the baby is mine.

CROCE *and* SIMONE *shake hands to clinch the deal. Night falls, the village empties.* MITA *comes forward in a nightdress, pale in the moonlight.* CROCE, TUZZA *and* SIMONE *dissipate.* MITA *sings out her melancholy.*

MITA (*singing*).
Day for day and night for night
It's all the same to me.
I live up in the grandest house
I couldn't care, not me.
A stranger in my life I am
The fig fell off its tree
An emerald pistachio
Dried and pale, is she.
Once I had some happy days
Away down past the hill
And happy nights pointing at stars
With him I dream of still.
Now I wake up filled with shame
At what's become of me
A paper doll, a marzipan ball,
A bird locked up, not free.
Day for day and night for night
It's all the same to me,
Day for day and night for night
Is all there seems to be.

MITA *speaks directly to us.*

Although the very next day proved more memorable than all the others.

She leaves. The space is empty. Day breaks. GESA comes forward with her chair, a large colander and LIOLÀ's three BOYS. She peels potatoes while the BOYS play, balancing on one leg.

CALICCHIO, PALLINO *and* TININO. We're flamingos!

It's early evening.

GESA. Which of you flamingos is the cleverest?

CALICCHIO. Me!

PALLINO. I'm clever.

GESA. Not Tinino?

TININO. Me.

CALICCHIO. I'm the cleverest.

PALLINO. No, I am.

CALICCHIO, PALLINO *and* TININO. It's me! – No, me! – You're stupid.

GESA. Come on now, all three, you're all clever in your way. But, we can't deny that Pallino is the oldest, so, Pallino, tell me, do you think you could pull up – see there, see where I mean…

PALLINO. Yes!

He runs off.

GESA. Wait! The onions.

CALICCHIO. I want to pick one.

TININO. And me.

GESA. Go on then, one onion each, but watch Pallino do it first.

CALICCHIO, PALLINO *and* TININO. Me first! – Why? – One each. – I know! (*Etc.*)

GESA. Just the three…

The BOYS return with an onion each.

Good lads. So, the rumours are true, flamingos are extremely clever birds.

NINFA *calls for them.*

NINFA. Pallino, Calicchio, Tinino!

GESA (*calling back*). They're with me, neighbour.

NINFA *comes on.*

NINFA. You buzz around here like flies, poor Aunt Gesa. Inside, now, the three of you.

GESA. They're no bother, Mother. They're my helpers, aren't you?

CALICCHIO, PALLINO *and* TININO. Yes! – Look! (*Etc.*)

NINFA. Well, if you're sure.

GESA. They're calm as anything in my little orchard, aren't you, boys?

NINFA. Just shoo them off if they become a nuisance.

She goes back.

GESA. If they're not calm, their father will – what will he do, what will Daddy do when he gets home?

CALICCHIO. He'll sing.

GESA. True, but what else, what does he do if you've been naughty for Grandma? Play the drums on your bottoms, no?

CIUZZA *appears.*

CIUZZA. Aunt Gesa, would you have a clove of garlic you could lend my mother, please?

GESA. Hello, Ciuzza, I do. Hanging in the kitchen, help yourself.

CIUZZA. Thank you, Aunt. Are they always with you, these boys? They're so lovely. Imagine not wanting to be their mother.

GESA. I see you wouldn't mind.

CIUZZA (*disingenuous*). What? I just meant they're easy to look after. (*Innocently.*) Where's their father this evening?

LUZZA *and* NELA *appear.*

LUZZA. Hey! Do you need any help, Aunt Gesa?

GESA. Hello, girls…

LUZZA (*to* NELA). Ciuzza's here already.

NELA. Do you have an extra knife?

GESA. You want to help, do you? God bless, what keen housewives all of a sudden. I have to tell you, though, he's not home yet.

NELA. Who?

GESA. Who could I possibly mean?

Crouching by GESA, *picking up a potato.*

LUZZA. I have my knife with me.

GESA. Not on the ground, Luzza, we're not that low. Pallino, fetch a chair, will you?

PALLINO *and* NELA *go.*

Steady there, Luzza, that's a sharp knife, you're cutting half the vegetable off.

LUZZA. Are we peeling them all?

GESA. Lord, no, it's just me, as ever. Two days' worth is plenty.

The others return with chairs.

It's a potato party, three girls to help me cook.

She starts a song, the others join in.

(*Singing.*)
Lo, there, lo there
Take the knife around…

GESA *and* GIRLS (*singing*).
>Cut the peel off
>Throw it on the ground.
>Throw it on the ground,
>Throw it on the ground,
>Cut the peel off
>Throw it on the ground.
>See him, see him,
>Who's the man for you?
>One day, he will
>Come for you and woo. (*Etc.*)

They carry on humming the song. Conversation continues over it.

GESA. I don't want your mother waiting on her garlic, Ciuzza...

CIUZZA. Oh, it's for this evening.

GESA. It's already this evening, which is why you hoped he'd be here.

CIUZZA. Who, Aunt Gesa?

GESA. The cat, young Ciuzza.

LUZZA. She knows who you mean.

GESA. I'm sharp, me.

CIUZZA. We were just wondering if it's true that Tuzza turned him down?

NELA. We heard it was her mother.

LUZZA (*to* GESA). What did you hear?

CIUZZA. I bet it was Tuzza.

NELA. But why would she say no when she's – (*Stopping herself.*) Stop it, Nela.

LUZZA. What does Liolà think, though?

CIUZZA. I say it serves him right.

LUZZA. Me too.

NELA. It does!

CIUZZA. He fancies all he needs to do is this – (*Her version of what* LIOLÀ *does*.) and girls throw themselves out of windows for him.

GESA (*dryly*). Really?

LUZZA. She doesn't mean us.

CIUZZA. Who cares about him?

LUZZA. We're interested, is all.

NELA. We want to hear what he's singing.

CIUZZA. He must be shocked.

LUZZA. Did you hear him last night?

GESA. Oh, stop, girls, what do you want? His mother is just across the way, go ask her!

NINFA *appears*.

NINFA. Sounds like the cicadas are out, Neighbour Gesa?

CIUZZA, LUZZA *and* NELA. Evening, Mother Ninfa. – Hello, Mother Ninfa. (*Privately*.) – She heard us… (*Etc*.)

GESA. Not cicadas, neighbour, but honeybees, that have fastened themselves to me. The girls are keen to know –

CIUZZA, LUZZA *and* NELA. No, we're not! – No! – We don't want to know anything! (*Etc*.)

GESA. They want to know if your son is singing songs of outrage because Tuzza Azzara / didn't accept his hand in marriage.

CIUZZA. We don't!

NELA. We don't want to know!

NINFA. Who says she didn't?

CIUZZA, LUZZA *and* NELA. Everybody. – He asked and she said no. – It's true.

NINFA. If it is true, she's done well, that Tuzza. Her mother has more sense than I thought. Were I mother to a daughter, I wouldn't give her to my son.

NELA. Does Liolà know you think that?

CIUZZA. Did you never have a daughter, Mother Ninfa?

NINFA. I had Liolà, that was that.

GESA. You know where he gets it from, don't you, girls?

NELA. No.

NINFA. Oh, don't, neighbour.

CIUZZA. Tell us!

NINFA. I'm an old woman!

CIUZZA, LUZZA *and* NELA. You're not that old. – No, you're not!

GESA. You can see she was a looker.

NINFA *can't resist, she postures as her younger self.*

NINFA. Nothing too special, I wasn't bad.

CIUZZA, LUZZA *and* NELA. Tell us. – What happened?

NINFA. There was a fight once, involving a number of young men.

GESA. Including Liolà's father.

CIUZZA, LUZZA *and* NELA. How many men? – Did he win? – What happened? – Hello!

NINFA. All I should say, girls, is don't be too sweet, lest you be eaten.

CIUZZA, LUZZA *and* NELA. What do you mean? – Don't stop there. – Tell us!

NINFA. We're talking about Liolà, and I'm giving you a warning – it's strong stuff, the Schillaci seed, protect yourselves. He has charms crafted in Hell, my son. The truth is, I wouldn't want him dallying with my dog. He does, I admit though, produce sweet children.

Her tone changes swiftly as the BOYS *encroach on them.*

You three, in the house, now!

CALICCHIO, PALLINO *and* TININO. Aw!

CÀRMINA (*off*). Gesa, Gesa? Oh, Jesus, Holy Jesus...

LUZZA. That's Càrmina.

NELA. What's she shouting for?

CÀRMINA *comes on.*

CÀRMINA. Gesa, Gesa.

NINFA. What's wrong, Càrmina?

CÀRMINA. The wreck in your niece's home.

GESA *stands, dropping her potatoes.*

GESA. Mita?

CÀRMINA. She's ruined, Gesa.

GESA. What's happened? Tell me, Càrmina.

CÀRMINA. She's wretched, wretched.

GESA. Oh, Mother of God, I have to go, I've got to see her.

She runs off.

CÀRMINA (*to* GESA, *as she goes*). Go, run, she's hysterical, wringing her hands like / Mary Magdalene.

CIUZZA, LUZZA *and* NELA. What's happened? – What is it?

NINFA. Has he hurt her?

CÀRMINA. That husband of hers, Uncle Simone... (*Stops.*)

CIUZZA, LUZZA *and* NELA. What?

NINFA. What is it?

CÀRMINA. It would seem he's been doing it with his cousin's daughter.

NINFA. No.

CIUZZA, LUZZA *and* NELA. What? – With Tuzza? – What do you mean?

CÀRMINA. With Tuzza. What's more, he's gone and got her...

She indicates pregnancy to NINFA.

NINFA. Mother of God, save us.

LUZZA *and* NELA. What? – I didn't see, what did she do?

CÀRMINA. Come on, girls, you're too young for this.

NELA. No we're not!

CÀRMINA. Away you go.

NINFA. Go on!

CIUZZA, LUZZA *and* NELA. Ach.

The GIRLS *retreat a short distance.*

NINFA (*to* CÀRMINA). Are you sure?

CÀRMINA. He's boasting to his own wife.

NINFA. How can he stoop so low.

CÀRMINA. Because, finally, he can prove that the problem wasn't his, but hers. He told Mita that if he'd married Tuzza instead, they'd have five children by now.

CIUZZA. Excuse me for interrupting, but – (*To* NINFA.) wasn't Tuzza together with Liolà until yesterday?

NINFA. I never know who he's with.

CÀRMINA. Don't play the innocent, Ninfa, you must know what he gets up to. Are we meant to believe that Simone has suddenly, miraculously, unearthed the power to make babies?

NINFA. I don't know what you're implying, Càrmina.

CÀRMINA. Oh, come on, you're telling me that Liolà has nothing to do with this?

NINFA. That's my son you're slandering.

CÀRMINA. Mother and daughter have put their heads together and duped the old man on the back of Liolà's tactics, I would cut both my hands off if it's not so.

CIUZZA. Me too.

LUZZA. Me too.

NELA. Everyone knows they were together.

NINFA. I don't.

CÀRMINA. Because you choose not to.

NINFA. Who are you, Càrmina, to throw accusations at me?

LUZZA. Mita's coming with her aunt!

MITA *and* GESA *come forward, distraught. The* GIRLS *tend to* MITA *while* GESA *paces, wracked with anger.*

GESA. My girl, my niece, may God strike him dead. He dared lay his filthy hands on her, the thug. After it all, such a miserable marriage, he attacks her, the butcher! He got hold of her hair and dragged her through their house. I'm going, I'm going to town – I'm leaving her here with you, neighbour. I'm going to shout for justice 'til I'm hoarse. Prison, prison, prison for that old criminal.

CÀRMINA. You tell them, Gesa, get yourself to the magistrate's.

NINFA. No, head for the lawyer's, mark my words.

GESA. I'll do both, I'll put him behind bars, the filthy fraudster. He had the nerve to say the child was his as sure as Christ's blood is in the cup at Holy Mass.

NINFA. Did he say that?

GESA. Prison, too, for that mother-and-daughter pair of whores! I'm going. It'll be night before I get there, I'll sleep at my sister's. You stay here, Mita, safe in the house. Lock the doors, both doors, there are potatoes peeled...

MITA. Thank you, Aunt.

GESA. Right, I'm going. Behind bars, the lot of them.

She goes, still shouting.

Damned rats, hussies…

All there is in the silence is MITA*'s barely contained grief.*

CÀRMINA (*trying to calm the atmosphere*). Separated, you can argue for him to pay your upkeep, Mita, don't worry.

NINFA. You want him to get away with it? You mustn't separate, you are his wife.

MITA. I'm not going back.

NINFA. But, Mita, what will become of you? That's just what they're wanting.

CÀRMINA. They'll take over your house, hand out garlic to his other relatives to munch on at his wake.

MITA. So I should go home and get beaten to death? I share nothing with him. He's got what he wanted from another woman and all three of them would like me dead.

CÀRMINA. They're strong words, Mita, but the law is stronger. Look, your aunt is halfway to town –

MITA. What can the law do? Five years I've stomached it. Do you know what he came this far from my face and shouted?

NELA. What?

MITA. 'Don't you dare speak badly of my niece.' Because his 'niece', he says, is an honest girl.

NINFA. He used that word?

CÀRMINA. That's unbelievable.

CIUZZA. 'Honest', ha!

LUZZA *and* NELA. Ha!

MITA. Because she's his girl now and he's going to leave her everything, because she's given him evidence, as he calls it, that it wasn't him who was lacking, but me. And that the law, in fact, should do something about poor men who find themselves hitched to barren sows like me. Mother Ninfa, I knew in my heart not to take him, I don't want his money! And I wouldn't have accepted if I felt I could have refused...

NINFA. Your aunt, I know...

MITA (*not defensive*). I was dependent on her.

CÀRMINA. You were without options.

MITA. I wanted to help my aunt, pay her back. Simone's so mean, she's had nothing so far.

CÀRMINA. You poor orphan.

MITA. I was happy here. My aunt's house, the orchard, you our neighbours... You must see the change in me, Mother. But I know God will find his way to punish those who have done me wrong.

CÀRMINA. Liolà has to speak out, Ninfa.

NINFA. Are you blaming him again, Càrmina?

CÀRMINA. Come on, girls, back me up.

CIUZZA, LUZZA *and* NELA. It was him! – We spied on them. – It's true, Mother Ninfa. – He even proposed to Tuzza!

MITA. I know that Liolà and I were good friends when I lived here, Mother, but I couldn't say no to that marriage.

NINFA. Mita, you don't think Liolà's done this to spite you, do you, after five years? He'd not do such a thing.

MITA. I hope not.

CÀRMINA. He wouldn't. But as a man of conscience, Mother, Liolà has to expose those contemptible cows or this innocent girl will be ruined.

They hear LIOLÀ *singing*.

LIOLÀ (*singing*).
> Every man I meet tells me the same,
> Once you take a wife,
> You have lost the game.

CÀRMINA. Speak of the Devil.

LUZZA. Liolà!

LIOLÀ (*singing*).
> Who wants to settle to a life like that,
> Who needs a wife?
> I'd rather have a cat.

CÀRMINA. I'll drill sense into him, Mita, don't you worry.

CIUZZA, LUZZA *and* NELA. Liolà!

NINFA. We're here, son.

CÀRMINA. In the orchard, Liolà.

LIOLÀ. Evening, Càrmina, how are you? It's the turtle doves.

He indicates the GIRLS, *they giggle.* LIOLÀ *is back in his ragged work clothes.*

CÀRMINA. Look who else is here.

LIOLÀ. Mita.

CÀRMINA. Poor Mita.

LIOLÀ. What's the matter, Mita?

CÀRMINA. Weeping over your misdoings.

LIOLÀ. Why, what have I done?

CÀRMINA. What haven't you done, Liolà, with Mother Croce's daughter.

LIOLÀ. Tuzza, what's she to do with this?

CÀRMINA. Everything. She and her mother, the devils, are claiming that the baby is Uncle Simone's.

LIOLÀ. Which baby?

CÀRMINA. Tuzza's baby.

LIOLÀ. No, really? Did Tuzza go and get herself –

He motions a pregnancy.

CIUZZA, LUZZA *and* NELA. Yes! – She's pregnant! – You know that!

NINFA. Away now, girls, off you go, this is no chat for you.

LUZZA. Oh, dear God, the same refrain – 'Off you go, you're too young...'

CIUZZA. We know everything already.

NELA. You're always saying things 'Not for our ears'.

LIOLÀ. I fear it's not for mine, either.

CÀRMINA (*to the* GIRLS). Are you three going? I cannot discuss this with you here.

CIUZZA. All right, we're leaving.

CIUZZA, LUZZA *and* NELA. Goodnight, Mother Ninfa. – Goodnight, Mita. – Goodnight, Càrmina.

CÀRMINA *and* NINFA. Goodnight.

LIOLÀ. Nothing for me?

CIUZZA. You're a bare-faced liar, Liolà.

LUZZA. You're bad blood.

They leave.

CÀRMINA. Tuzza's baby is yours, Liolà, and you know it.

LIOLÀ. Oh, stop, will you? You're sounding like a busybody, Càrmina.

CÀRMINA. Thanks.

LIOLÀ. You're too intelligent for that, and young. I, of all people, know how young you are.

CÀRMINA. Stop it, Liolà, you hold nothing on me.

LIOLÀ. I know, Càrmina. So what are these accusations? I get the blame for the slightest misadventure round here. A girl's mouth starts watering, 'It must be Liolà'.

CÀRMINA. Are you denying it?

LIOLÀ. Of course I am, I know nothing about it.

CÀRMINA. Then why did you ask Mother Croce for Tuzza's hand?

LIOLÀ. I was wondering how I got roped in.

CÀRMINA. You see, Mother Ninfa, he did propose.

LIOLÀ. For a joke.

CÀRMINA. A joke?

LIOLÀ. A passing impulse.

CÀRMINA. You speak to him, you're his mother. He blows hot air at me while there's an innocent girl in shreds. Where's your loyalty gone, Liolà? Look at her.

LIOLÀ (to MITA). It breaks my heart to see your tears, but tell me why, Mita?

CÀRMINA. 'Why', he asks? Speak to him, Mother.

NINFA. Because, Uncle Simone –

CÀRMINA. Now you're talking –

NINFA. It sounds like –

CÀRMINA. Sounds like? He pulled her through the house by her hair!

NINFA. He claims he's having this baby with Tuzza.

LIOLÀ. For mercy's sake, Uncle Simone with his cousin?

NINFA. See? My son is sincere.

CÀRMINA. And we're supposed to swallow this? You, who have never been in the least bit inclined to marry anyone –

LIOLÀ. How would you know, Càrmina?

CÀRMINA. Even when you were young and in love –

LIOLÀ. It's the opposite.

CÀRMINA. Oh, here we go, your charity cases…

LIOLÀ. What can I do if they turn me down? I've no guilt.

CÀRMINA. How so?

LIOLÀ. I offer marriage wholeheartedly, but nobody wants me. Or they do, for half an hour. If I had a priest in those minutes, I could have had a number of wives. But back to the business of Tuzza, well done, Simone, the old cockerel's done it at last.

CÀRMINA. Like hell he has.

LIOLÀ. Don't take it from him, Càrmina – what a man, looks past it but is clearly not. Tuzza can expect to be treated like a princess now – do you remember that huge wedding reception he threw for you, Mita...?

(*To* MITA, *a sudden gentleness.*) Don't take it too hard. However you're feeling, the fact is, what can you do?

CÀRMINA. You're bringing on a heart attack here, I have to leave. I've not the years left in me to wrestle conscience-dodgers like you.

NINFA. That's enough, Càrmina, accusing my boy.

But CÀRMINA*'s going. She shouts back to* MITA.

CÀRMINA. I'm sorry, Mita, I can't stay.

NINFA *shouts after her.*

NINFA. Are you so dull as to think that everything is just as you imagine it?

CÀRMINA *shouts back at them.*

CÀRMINA. I hope neither of you sleeps a wink tonight!

She's gone.

LIOLÀ. Don't rise to it, Mother. Let's get these lads to bed. Look, Tinino's asleep already.

The BOYS *have crept forward while the adults talked.* TININO *is flat on the ground, asleep, the other two are dropping off where they sit.*

NINFA. So he is. (*Gently calling.*) Tinino? Tinino.

He doesn't wake.

We'll have to carry him, little man.

LIOLÀ *lifts* TININO *up. He whistles to rouse the other two. They blearily stand up and follow him off.*

LIOLÀ (*singing*).
Little, little lullaby,
Child of mine, sleepy eye,
Little, little lullaby
Beddy-byes is nigh.

MITA. I'd best get in, too. Goodnight, Mother Ninfa.

NINFA. If you need me, daughter, as soon as the boys are down, I'll come back and be with you.

MITA. Thank you, but I'm locking up and going straight to bed.

NINFA. If you're sure, Mita. I'm here if you change your mind.

MITA. Thank you, Mother Ninfa.

NINFA. Get yourself some rest, love.

NINFA *goes.*

MITA. Goodnight, Liolà.

Beat. He turns back, the sleeping TININO *still in his arms.*

LIOLÀ. Are you stopping here tonight?

MITA. Yes.

LIOLÀ. Where's your aunt?

MITA. In town, seeing the lawyer.

LIOLÀ. You don't want to go back to him?

MITA. Why would I? Goodnight.

LIOLÀ. That's not wise, Mita.

MITA. We can't all be as sanguine as you, Liolà. I have to trust in God now.

LIOLÀ. Because he's supposed to take care of everything? Maybe he did in the old days, Mita, but good as you are, as respectful of the Holy Commandments, you can't expect the Virgin Mary treatment.

MITA. You blasphemer, I don't.

LIOLÀ. How else can God help, if not through His Holy Spirit?

MITA. Go home, Liolà. Tinino needs his bed and I can't stay listening to your heresies.

LIOLÀ. Heresies?

(*Calling inside.*) Mother?

NINFA. Son?

LIOLÀ. Would you mind taking Tinino up?

MITA. I have to go in, Liolà.

LIOLÀ. Mita, wait!

He passes TININO *over to* NINFA*, she takes him off,* LIOLÀ *hurries back.*

It's not heresy, it's reality. You can't expect God to help in that particular way.

MITA. I know, I don't!

LIOLÀ. So how come I'm the heretic? You have to ask, what other help is there? Càrmina kicking off, or your aunt dragging the lawyer in? Sending me to holler in Simone's face that Tuzza's baby is mine? It's gnat's play, Mita. They're the kind of solutions we found as children, arguing in this orchard, running to tell our side of the story to your aunt or my mother... do you remember?

MITA. Of course I do. It wasn't what I wanted, Liolà, I just said so to your mother. God knew where my heart was when I walked down that aisle.

LIOLÀ. I know it, Mita. I was no contender. The fact is, you're married, and that's that.

MITA (*embarrassed*). I only mention it because you asked if I remembered.

LIOLÀ. Mita, you are wrong and your husband is right.

MITA. How am I wrong?

LIOLÀ. How long have you been married?

MITA. Five years.

LIOLÀ. That's how you're wrong. Five years. He's tired. You knew that he was marrying you for children, and have you any? He waited and waited and in the end did the only thing he could, found someone else to give him babies.

MITA. It was not God's will that I had children!

LIOLÀ. It's not God's will that it rains lemons. You call it God yet you say I blaspheme? Go ask Tuzza who made her pregnant, Mita.

MITA. The Devil did.

LIOLÀ. No, it was Uncle Simone.

MITA. You and I both know that's not true.

LIOLÀ. It's your husband's child.

MITA. How can you stand there saying that, Liolà?

LIOLÀ. You're just not thinking straight, Mita.

MITA. And you're clear-sighted as ever, aren't you? Things don't cost you, Liolà.

This stabs him.

LIOLÀ. Do they not, Mita? Say I do spread the word all over town, go to Uncle Simone with a goat-bell round my neck, 'Dang, dang, I'm the father, I'm the father', who'll believe me? Some, certainly, maybe even everyone – but not him.

MITA. Why not?

LIOLÀ. Uncle Simone would never believe that baby's mine because he wants it. And will the child be born with a sign on his forehead saying, 'Liolà's'? No. Mothers are blind when they want to be, so, fathers… they'll believe anything. And if no other man claims it, Simone can persuade himself that it honestly is his.

MITA. How?

LIOLÀ. What'll he tell himself? That he was drunk and forgot going with his cousin, that the child was grace-given by God? Who knows. But until his death he'll claim it as his and nothing I can do would dissuade him. So you, Mita, of all people, have to go along with the idea that it is definitely –

MITA. His child?

LIOLÀ *affirms this.*

LIOLÀ. Reassure him that all this time it wasn't him lacking, it was you, and isn't it wonderful that he's having a child with Tuzza.

Beat.

Because it means that, tomorrow, he can have one with his wife.

MITA. What are you talking about, Liolà?

They're speaking very quietly.

LIOLÀ. Do you not understand me, Mita? He can have a child with you the same way he's having one with Tuzza.

MITA. Which way?

LIOLÀ. Nature's way.

MITA. No. Dear God, no.

LIOLÀ. Goodnight, then. Dry your tears and stop complaining, because who else is going to help? I've shown you the perfect way. It's probably the way God took with his precious Mary all those years ago.

MITA. Stop it, Liolà!

LIOLÀ. I just meant nature knows best. And I'm choked up because you would rather let Tuzza ruin your life than take a risk on what comes after, which none of us knows because none of us is dead yet.

MITA. Your tongue...

LIOLÀ. Fine, I'll leave, but what else are you going to do? I've denied the baby for you, Mita, because there is no other way back from that deceit – crooked wood is straightened with fire. And if you think it's just you getting hurt, you're wrong. I'm biting my tongue here, it's painful.

He's got her attention again.

When I went to ask Tuzza to marry me, her mother wheedled your husband into the house where Tuzza was waiting. I witnessed it, their moment of betrayal. All I could think of was you, Mita. I saw, like a painting, what would happen, exactly as it has, and I promised myself that I wouldn't let them win. So I sealed my lips, and was waiting for just such a moment as this. Don't give in, Mita. You have the power to right a wrong and punish the betrayers, which is unarguably what God himself would do, isn't it? I won't let them use me to ruin you.

He finally touches her, gently. She draws in to him, lifts her face to his. As they become more passionate, she throws him off, untangles herself.

MITA. Leave me, please, I can't do this!

He tries again.

LIOLÀ. Mita...

MITA. I don't want to, I'm married, I'm a married woman...

She stops still, terrified.

Ssh, there's someone coming! (*Calling.*) Who is it?

(*Whispering to* LIOLÀ.) I'm sure that's his step. Run, Liolà, for heaven's sake!

LIOLÀ *hides in the shadows.* SIMONE *appears with a small lantern.*

SIMONE. Aunt Gesa? Aunt Gesa?

MITA. What do you want?

SIMONE. Mita?

MITA. Go away.

SIMONE. I want to speak to you.

MITA. Leave me alone.

SIMONE. I won't.

MITA *passes him, calling for* NINFA. *He grabs her.*

MITA. Aunt Ninfa? Get off me.

SIMONE. You're behaving like a child.

MITA *shakes* SIMONE *off.*

MITA (*calling*). Neighbour Ninfa?

LIOLÀ *listens intently in the dark.*

(*To* SIMONE.) What are you doing here?

SIMONE. Taking you home.

SIMONE *puts his lantern down and grabs her with both hands. For the first time,* MITA *is fighting back.*

MITA. Get off! (*Calling.*) Mother Ninfa? (*To* SIMONE.) I'm not coming.

SIMONE. But you're my wife.

MITA. And you're a bully. (*Calling.*) Mother Ninfa, Neighbour Ninfa?

SIMONE. Why are you calling for help, for goodness' sake?

NINFA *hurries from the back.*

NINFA. Mita, love, are you all right? Ah, Uncle Simone, it's you.

SIMONE. Good evening, Mother Ninfa.

MITA. Tell him to go, Mother.

SIMONE. I've come to fetch her home.

MITA. You've come to the wrong place. You should be at the home of that low-down cousin of yours!

SIMONE. Be quiet now, or you'll feel the weight of my hand.

NINFA. Hey, that's enough, Uncle Simone, give her time to cool off, for goodness' sake.

SIMONE. She should show some respect. If she can't be a mother, the least she can be is a decent wife.

NINFA. Let's be fair, Simone, she's reeling from what you've done.

SIMONE. And what have I done, besides pick her off the street, virtually, and place her in a house too good for her to live in.

NINFA. Bless you, man, you think that's the way to get a girl to come home with you?

SIMONE. Mother Ninfa, I'm a good Christian, but I have had nobody to leave my money to, which I have earned through the sweat of my brow in sun, rain and hail, and now, at last, I have a child.

NINFA. Well, good for you, but where's Mita's blame in that?

SIMONE. It's not her fault entirely, and I wouldn't have treated my first wife that way, but neither should Mita attack the person who managed to do the thing she couldn't.

MITA (*to* NINFA). Do you hear that?

(*To* SIMONE, *who is trying to grab her again*.) What do you want with me? Go to her who's done the thing and leave me in peace.

SIMONE. You don't understand, she is my relative, you are my wife.

MITA. Exactly!

SIMONE. What happened, happened, we won't speak of it again, but I need a woman in the house and that must be my wife.

MITA. I would rather throw myself under a moving cart than be that woman.

NINFA. Uncle Simone, the blow you've dealt is too strong, be patient. Mita will calm down and then she'll come home.

MITA. Wait all you like, I'm never going back.

NINFA. He's come all this way and he's told you it's finished, that he won't go to Mother Croce's any more – (*To* SIMONE.) isn't that right?

SIMONE. I won't, Mother. When the baby's born it'll live in my house.

MITA. And then its mother will come and treat me like dirt, a servant.

NINFA. Why would she?

MITA. Could I shut the door on Tuzza and Croce? Mother Ninfa, you wouldn't have the heart to pack me off to that, would you?

NINFA. What's it got to do with me, sweet girl? Just, for your own good, you should go with your husband.

SIMONE (*to* MITA). Come on now, it's dark.

MITA. No! If you don't leave me, I will run and throw myself off the bridge!

NINFA. Uncle, listen, why don't you leave her here for the night. Hopefully, tomorrow, she'll soften, regain some judgement. What I feel in my bones is that she'll be back with you by tomorrow night.

SIMONE. Then why stay tonight?

NINFA. Gently, bit by bit. It's late, go home, get some sleep. (*To* MITA.) Show your husband to the path now, Mita, then get back inside your aunt's house and lock up for the night. Have a good rest, both of you.

MITA *and* SIMONE *go, forgetting* SIMONE*'s lantern.* NINFA *sees* LIOLÀ.

(*Whispering*.) Go home, son, don't create madness here…

LIOLÀ (*whispering*). Shh, I want to see how it ends. Go in, Mother, go to sleep.

NINFA. Have sense, will you.

LIOLÀ. I do.

She goes. LIOLÀ *comes out of the shadows, waits.* MITA *comes into the orchard. They look at one another.* SIMONE *shouts.*

SIMONE. Mita?

MITA *runs towards* LIOLÀ, *they hide in the shadows together.*

I left my lantern in the orchard.

He gropes his way back to the orchard.

It's so dark, you know how I hate the dark. I feel I'll trip and crack my head with every step.

SIMONE *sees his lantern, falls on it.*

Thank the Lord for light, it restores good sense to a slippery world.

Shouts, presuming she's inside.

Goodnight, wife. I'll see you tomorrow.

He leaves. The MUSICIANS *quietly begin playing.* MITA *and* LIOLÀ *emerge. The space between them is highly charged. Slowly, they dance together.* LIOLÀ *carries* MITA *off.*

CÀRMINA *comes forward.*

CÀRMINA (*singing*).
    Easy to see me
    Think it's a choice
    But why would I choose it,
    Having no voice?
    Mayoress of a city
    Not working the land

A lawyer, but pretty
My dreams built on sand
Built on sand.
Being boss of the vineyards
Not picking grapes,
Selling the nuts
Not manning the rakes
I rail at my neighbours,
Hear myself bitch at my dog,
Scorn for each newlywed,
Scorn for the rich, what a hog.

GESA *and* NINFA *join the song.*

GESA *and* NINFA (*singing*).
That's how it is, that's how it is, that's how it is, how
it is, that's how. That's how it is, that's how it is,
that's how it is, that's how.

CÀRMINA (*singing*).
All the young girls
Think I am old,
Pedantic and bracing
Unfeeling and cold.
He went to mainland
Never came back
I wanted to put my
Head in a sack.
Brains for no reason
Body still free
All of the island
Hooked, but not me.

GESA *and* NINFA (*singing*).
That's how it is, that's how it is, that's how it is, how it is,
that's how. That's how it is, that's how it is, that's how it
is, that's how.

CÀRMINA (*singing*).
Brains for no reason
Body still free

All of the island
Hooked, but not me.

WHOLE VILLAGE (*singing*).
That's how it is, that's how it is, that's how it is, how
it is, that's how. That's how it is, that's how it is,
that's how it is, that's how.

All the village is back, gathered together once again.

CÀRMINA (*speaking to us*). Tuzza's belly grew all summer
until it stared you in the face. (*Indicating* CROCE *and*
TUZZA.) No one went near them if they could possibly help
it. Mita returned to her husband, kept her head down, that's
how it is.

The day brightens to a September day, back outside
CROCE*'s house. Empty baskets are piled up.* TUZZA, *eight*
months pregnant, sews a baby outfit. CROCE *covers her*
head with a handkerchief. They wait.

CROCE. They're rolling in gold, suddenly, are they? Where are
they all?

TUZZA. I don't know why you're surprised.

CROCE. We're not asking them to sit at table with us. They live
like dogs without enough straw to sleep on, but when I invite
them to earn an honest crust, Luzza's pulled her shoulder
out, so-and-so's hurt her leg...

TUZZA. Let them starve, don't go begging.

CROCE. It's envy. They pass here stiff as broomsticks because
they're jealous. It's a waste for our few vines but I'll have to
go to town, find some labour over for harvest, if we don't
want the grapes ravaged by wasps. Is the press ready?

TUZZA. It's ready.

CROCE. All set then, minus the workers.

Beat.

He's the only one who promised to come.

TUZZA. Who?

CROCE. Liolà.

TUZZA. Did you have to ask him?

CROCE. Of course I did, to show that there's nothing going on.

TUZZA. Even the stones know by now.

CROCE. Not from him, to be fair, he denies it each time. I don't know why. I'm not saying I'm not grateful, because if Liolà disowns it, everyone else can go chatter to the wind.

TUZZA. I'm warning you, when he comes I'm locking myself in the house, I can't bear to see him.

CROCE. Now you can't, bit late, isn't it?

TUZZA. All right. It's turned out for the best, hasn't it?

CROCE. I wonder where your uncle's been.

TUZZA. He sent Fillicò to say he wasn't well.

CROCE. Handsome Fillicò?

TUZZA. Married Fillicò.

CROCE. This child will be born, it will be born, and next year this grape harvest won't be our responsibility, it'll be his! It's going to be so different. Simone will choose the baby's name in front of his wife and everyone. He'll probably end up living with us, because home is where the children are.

CÀRMINA *appears, excited.*

CÀRMINA. Am I the first?

CROCE (*surprised*). You are, Càrmina, truly.

CÀRMINA. The others are on their way, all of them.

CROCE. They told me they couldn't come. You're glowing, Càrmina.

CÀRMINA. I'm happy, Mother Croce, I'm feeling really uplifted.

CROCE. You're red as a pepper, did you run?

CÀRMINA. I always run, too fast, sometimes, but you know what they say, 'The hen that runs like a bull, keeps its belly full.' It's harvest time, everyone's festive.

CROCE. It wasn't that way earlier.

TUZZA. Don't give them the work, I wouldn't.

CÀRMINA. You wouldn't, would you, Tuzza.

TUZZA. I'd go to town, get new workers.

CROCE. I'm not one to perpetuate bad blood between neighbours.

CÀRMINA. Are you not?

CROCE. I'm pleased the hard feelings are done with, but I'd like to know why everyone's so happy, suddenly.

CÀRMINA. Maybe it's because they know Liolà is helping. He's unique, Mother, I think he made a pact with Satan.

CROCE. What's he done now?

CÀRMINA. I can barely fathom it, but the fact is he brings joy to our hearts. He does one thing, but thinks of a hundred.

Music starts up.

Here he is, a crowd with him. Always a song, and his little ones jumping round…

LIOLÀ*'s gypsy band has swelled to its fullest.* CIUZZA, LUZZA, NELA, PALLINO, CALICCHIO, TININO, NINFA *and others sing with him, a harvest song they know, stamping and dancing as they walk.*

LIOLÀ *and* OTHERS (*singing*).
Ni-na na-na ni-na na na
Ni-na na-na ni-na na na
Stompa stompa stompa stompa
Stomp stomp stomp
Ni-na na-na ni-na na na

> Ni-na na-na ni-na na na
> Stompa stompa stompa stompa
> Stomp stomp stomp
> Burst the grapes, burst the grapes,
> Burst the grapes, burst the grapes,
> Down down down down
> Down down down down down.

EVERYONE (*singing*).

> Ni-na na-na ya-no, ni-na na-na ya-no
> Ni-na na-na ni-na na na, ni-na na-na ni-na na na
> Ni-na na-na ni-na na na, ni-na ya-na no. (*Repeat.*)

LIOLÀ *and* OTHERS (*singing*).

> Fill the drum
> Make us young, make us young
> Feel our beating hearts take flight
> Make us dance through the night
> Drink a barrel full of red wine
> Drink a barrel full of white wine
> Drink a barrel full of red wine
> Drink a barrel full of white wine
> Down down down down
> Down down down down down.

EVERYONE (*singing*).

> Ni-na na-na ya-no, ni-na na-na ya-no
> Ni-na na-na ni-na na na, ni-na na-na ni-na na na
> Ni-na na-na ni-na na na, ni-na ya-na...
> Ni-na na-na ya-no, ni-na na-na ya-no
> Ni-na na-na ni-na na na, ni-na na-na ni-na na na
> Ni-na na-na ni-na na na, ni-na ya-na no.

During the song, LIOLÀ *hands out all the empty baskets.*

LIOLÀ. We're here, Mother Croce.

CROCE. So I see.

LIOLÀ. You have the baskets?

Everyone is boisterous. TUZZA *leaves.*

Tuzza, Angelo's here.

CÀRMINA. Angelo's married, Liolà, Tuzza wouldn't tangle with a married man…

CROCE. Why all this glee, what miracle's occurred?

LIOLÀ. No miracle, Mother, just the sure path of nature taking its course. 'Endurance pierces marble', you know that one?

CIUZZA, LUZZA *and* NELA *laugh uncontrollably.*

CROCE. What are you talking about, Liolà?

LIOLÀ. It's just a proverb.

CROCE. Oh, and do you know this one, 'talk and song, to the wind belong'?

LIOLÀ. Or, you, this? 'Don't quote your proverb 'til your ship's in port'?

CROCE. Talking of ships, let's get these grapes in. Everybody all right on last year's agreement?

Beat.

LIOLÀ. Hoist your sails, everyone.

CROCE. Handle the fruit gently, you know the form.

LIOLÀ. I brought the children for any loose grapes.

CROCE. So long as they don't climb the trestle.

LIOLÀ. They've been taught at the school of their father, Mother Croce, if you can't reach a fruit, leave it on the tree. It might be sweeter for waiting.

The GIRLS *laugh. Looking at* CROCE'*s face.*

Is the press ready to go?

CROCE. Yes, all set.

LIOLÀ. Everyone got a basket? Come on then.

(*Singing.*)
    Down down down down.

Everyone joins in.

EVERYONE (*singing*).
> Down down down down
> Down
> Ni-na na-na ya-no,
> Ni-na na-na ya-no,
> Ni-na na-na ni-na na na,
> Ni-na na-na ni-na na na
> Ni-na na-na ni-na na na
> Na-na ya-na no.

They go off singing, to fill their baskets. CROCE *shouts after them.*

CROCE. Work upwards, row by row, and keep an eye on the little ones!

TUZZA *comes back.*

Stir your stumps, you, must I look after every last thing on my own? Get down there with them.

TUZZA. I told you, I'm not going.

CROCE. Who do you think you are to pick and choose? In the old days, I couldn't get you out the field with all those men in it.

TUZZA (*her pregnancy*). Look at me, Mother!

CROCE. You're good for nothing. I'll go myself, I don't trust those bloodsuckers, did you see the look in their eyes? Flames blazing in them.

TUZZA. I saw.

CROCE. Oh, here's your uncle, at last. Dragging his legs like tree trunks.

SIMONE *comes forward.*

SIMONE. Dear cousin, how are you, and Tuzza, I trust you're well?

TUZZA. I'm fine, thank you, Uncle. Are you better?

CROCE. Can I get you a seat, cousin?

She offers him her chair.

SIMONE. We have problems, cousin.

CROCE. Have you seen my almond trees? They're looking very healthy this year.

SIMONE. It's not the almonds.

CROCE. What problems do you have, cousin?

SIMONE. It's not exactly I, myself, that has problems.

CROCE. Is Mita sick?

SIMONE. In a way, yes, in another way, no.

CROCE *loses her polite patience.*

CROCE. Cousin, there are pickers in the vineyard, I have to keep my eye on them.

SIMONE. You've started harvest already?

CROCE. The grapes, just, they've gone down this minute.

SIMONE. Without telling me?

CROCE. You've not shown your face for three days. I've been battling with these vipers. First, they don't want to know, then they descend on us with dancing eyes. I want to kill them.

SIMONE. That's you all over, cousin, rash.

CROCE. Rash? The wasps are swarming the vines.

SIMONE. I'm not talking about the grapes, other things, too, I mean, me as well. I don't know what the hurry is, we don't let time take its course.

CROCE. Lord knows what your point is, cousin. Clearly you have a bone to pick with me.

SIMONE. The only bone I'm picking is with myself, cousin.

CROCE. For what?

SIMONE. Those who wait at the ferry, will eventually cross the water.

CROCE. What is it with boats, today?

SIMONE. Does the burden I'm carrying look light to you? Last night, Neighbour Randisi came to see me.

CROCE. I saw him pass.

SIMONE. Did he stop to say hello?

CROCE. No, straight by, as ever.

TUZZA. Everybody passes us.

SIMONE *seizes his moment*.

SIMONE. They pass by, my dear, because people... they imagine what, by the grace of God, is not the reality. Our consciences are clear, niece, but, unfortunately, the appearance isn't optimal.

CROCE. We know that, Uncle Simone.

TUZZA. Soon to be Father Simone...

CROCE. We've always known. We expected no less of these envious people. (*To* TUZZA.) You can hardly complain now, girl.

SIMONE. The problem is, cousin, that all those people who blank you with silence, walk up to my house and hector me.

CROCE. Come on, spill the beans, what has that devil, Randisi, been saying?

SIMONE. He was the one that said the thing about the ferry, 'Those who wait at the – '

CROCE (*interrupting*). Yes, all right –

SIMONE (*carrying on*). He also told me and told my wife, that there have been cases where couples, not only after five years but after fifteen years of marriage, suddenly find themselves with child.

CROCE. Oh? I was wondering what he could have said to put you in so pensive a mood. So tell me, cousin, what did you say back? You're sixty-five, no? Let's say you've had five of those fifteen years already in your marriage, so add another ten on top of that, makes seventy-five, right, cousin? Are you saying it's 'no' at sixty-five but 'yes' at seventy-five?

SIMONE. Well, who says it's 'no' at sixty-five, cousin?

CROCE. It's fact, cousin.

SIMONE. In fact, the fact is, cousin...

He hesitates to finish his sentence.

CROCE. What, cousin?

SIMONE. That it's 'yes' at sixty-five.

The WOMEN *are stunned.*

CROCE. I beg your pardon?

TUZZA. I don't believe this.

CROCE. Your wife?

SIMONE. She broke it to me this morning.

Long beat.

TUZZA. Liolà. I hate him.

CROCE. It's him, cousin, Liolà is the one who's done this.

SIMONE. Ladies, ladies, let's not jump to saying bitter things.

TUZZA. That's why they were laughing, the bitches!

CROCE. Do you dare to believe, cousin, that the child is yours?

TUZZA. 'Endurance pierces marble', the murdering –

CROCE. Is that how you keep watch over your wife, imbecile?

TUZZA. He's done it to her like he's done to me!

SIMONE. This is not the right response, ladies.

TUZZA. I told you to guard against him, Uncle. 'Watch out for Liolà,' I kept saying. You knew he liked your wife!

SIMONE. For the love of God, will you wipe Liolà's name off your lips! Remember when my wife said the same about you I defended you, although it was perfectly true.

CROCE. But now it's not? You old cuckold.

SIMONE. Cousin, you'd do well to shut your mouth.

CROCE. Don't threaten me, cousin. He can't get at a girl without her consent, that's the truth.

SIMONE. I know what the truth is.

CROCE. You just won't face it!

SIMONE. The truth is, cousin, that I have shared five years of marriage with my wife but never shared a thing of that nature with your daughter. She used to sit on Madalena's and my knees as a child, for goodness' sake. I did an act of charity here, nothing more.

CROCE. Ha!

SIMONE. With Mita, however, I was there, we were there, we didn't give up!

CROCE. When were you there? For five fruitless years, that's when. Who was there when it counted, Simone?

TUZZA. Did you call me an act of charity?

CROCE. He did, after boasting to the wide world that your baby was his.

SIMONE. Circumstances have changed, cousin.

CROCE. You took all the glory, all the credit, knowing full well the child wasn't yours, because you knew it was your only chance.

TUZZA. Stop it, Mother, the shouting's giving me a headache.

CROCE. What are you saying, girl – give up?

TUZZA. If he accepted my baby as his, knowing it meant that Liolà's child would inherit his fortune, do you honestly think he won't accept his own wife's baby?

SIMONE. Mita's child is mine. My wife is having our baby, ours, and I'll deal strongly with anybody who utters a word against her.

MITA *comes, calm, unflustered, accompanied by* GESA.

CROCE. Here she comes, look.

MITA. What's all the commotion?

TUZZA. Get away from here, Mita, don't test me.

GESA. She, test you?

MITA. God spare us that, Tuzza, surely.

TUZZA *lunges at* MITA, SIMONE *protects his wife*.

TUZZA. Get her out of my sight!

GESA. Keep back, you little trout.

SIMONE. It's all right, I'm here, I'm dealing with this.

CROCE. Go away, Mita. You have the boldness to show your face here?

MITA. Boldness, Mother Croce? You can talk.

SIMONE (*to* MITA). Don't get mixed up in these things, my dear, go home.

CROCE. Do as your husband says, make yourself scarce.

MITA. I'm going.

GESA. If this is the welcome we get.

MITA. I'd just like to remind you, Tuzza, that where you went, I followed.

TUZZA. Too right you did, up the exact same street.

MITA. No, my street's straight and clear, your road is twisted.

SIMONE. Go home, Mita, they're saying these things to goad you.

GESA. They are.

SIMONE. Trust me, sweet wife, go home now. And you, Aunt.

CROCE. 'Sweet wife', will you hear that.

TUZZA. It makes me sick. You have all the certificates, all I had were words.

MITA. Just words? I don't think so.

SIMONE. Come now, ladies.

CROCE. Yes, words, they make a paler lie than yours. The deceit here isn't where it seems to be, it's in you, where the look of it is invisible.

SIMONE. Have you finished, have we finished here?

CROCE. Deceitful, yet you have your husband's blessing. My daughter didn't want to deceive her cousin, she threw herself at his feet and told him the truth.

SIMONE. That is true.

CROCE. Even he admits it. It was him went boasting about the child, crowing to everyone.

MITA. And you let him, Mother Croce, to your family's shame. She told him the truth, did she? That you and she wanted your hands on all my husband's money – is that what she told him?

GESA. That you planned to take what wasn't yours to have.

SIMONE. That's enough, we are all family here. Instead of wasting breath on these accusations, let's calm down and come to some sensible arrangement.

CROCE. Looking for a way out now, you old fool, after damaging our reputation by trumpeting it to the whole town? So, family, cousin, what's your remedy?

SIMONE (*to* TUZZA). I was trying to help you, but now I have a child of my own to consider. Yours has his own father to worry about him. Liolà can't possibly deny now, under this new set of circumstances, that the child is his.

TUZZA. Which one?

This stings like nothing so far.

SIMONE. Just what do you mean by that?

MITA (*quickly*) Yours, Tuzza, who else's?

GESA. Who else's?

SIMONE (*to* TUZZA *and* CROCE). That's enough or I will disown you once and for all.

MITA. I am married and my husband has never had cause to doubt me.

SIMONE (*to* TUZZA *and* CROCE). My wife has brought me this precious gift and I do not want it poisoned by you.

They hear singing. Everybody arrives with their baskets full of grapes. The evening is drawing in, lamps are lit.

EVERYONE (*singing*).
Drink a barrel full of red wine
Drink a barrel full of white wine
Drink a barrel full of red wine
Drink a barrel full of white wine
Down down down down
Down down down down down.

As they notice the thick atmosphere, one by one they stop singing, apart from LIOLÀ.

LIOLÀ (*singing*).
Ni-na na-na ya-no, ni-na na-na ya-no
Ni-na na-na ni-na na na, ni-na na-na ni-na na na
Ni-na na-na ni-na na na, ni-na ya-na no.

CROCE (*dark*). Put the baskets down and leave.

LIOLÀ. What's the matter, Mother Croce?

CROCE. I'm not in the mood for socialising.

(*To the* GIRLS.) I said, go!

SIMONE. Not you, Liolà, you stay.

CIUZZA, LUZZA *and* NELA *crowd round* MITA. TUZZA *watches them.*

CIUZZA, LUZZA *and* NELA. How many weeks are you? – You look gorgeous! – You give us hope, Mita! – See you later! (*Etc.*)

TUZZA. Luzza, could I borrow your knife?

LUZZA *gives it to her. The* GIRLS *leave* MITA.

GESA (*to* SIMONE). My niece needs to sit down in her condition, Uncle Simone, may she have your seat?

CÀRMINA. See you, Mita. Goodbye, Tuzza.

She heads off too. LIOLÀ *looks at* MITA. *A vulnerable smile can't avoid escaping from her.* TUZZA *sees it.*

SIMONE. Liolà.

LIOLÀ (*to* SIMONE). Did you want me?

CROCE *gathers the baskets.*

SIMONE (*to* CROCE). Cousin, you too.

CROCE *stops her work. She and* TUZZA *hang back from the conversation.*

(*To* LIOLÀ.) Today is a very special day.

LIOLÀ. Sounds like a song might be in keeping.

SIMONE. No.

LIOLÀ. No? Mother Croce says songs are just so much air, but then I think the wind is my brother.

SIMONE. We know, Liolà, you are breezy and weightless, but you are also flesh and blood, which is what I want to talk to you about.

LIOLÀ (*starting up a song*).
   My flesh is young
   My blood is wild
   Warm enough
   To make a child…

SIMONE. Hush, will you, long enough for me to share my good fortune.

LIOLÀ *stops, so does the band.*

God has finally favoured me with –

CROCE (*to* LIOLÀ). Are you listening, you who played no part?

SIMONE (*to* CROCE). Would you leave the talking to me.

CROCE. Don't let me stop you.

SIMONE. Thank you.

CROCE. Tell us again how God brings you this heavenly gift.

SIMONE. As Mother Croce says, finally, after five years of trying –

LIOLÀ. Really?

SIMONE. My wife and I –

LIOLÀ. Mita?

Turning to MITA.

SIMONE. For the love of God, wait, I've not finished!

LIOLÀ. I just want to congratulate my old friend. (*To* MITA.) I'll make you a song, Mita.

(*Singing.*)
     We've known each other so long, so long, so long –

SIMONE. That's as may be, but you have something you must do first.

LIOLÀ. Me? All I'm fit for is farming and singing.

CROCE. Doesn't know about anything else, poor lamb.

She grabs him, quiet and vicious.

That's a grand total of twice you've ruined my daughter.

LIOLÀ. Are you mad, Mother Croce, with Simone standing here? He's your man, how can you say it's me?

CROCE. Oh, how could it possibly be you?

LIOLÀ. You, of all people, accuse me? Let's not go changing our hand mid-game, Croce. It's Simone, it's always been Simone. I came, in good faith, to ask for your daughter's hand and you turned me down. I had no idea she was –

CROCE. After what you did with her?

LIOLÀ. You mean after what Uncle Simone did with her.

CROCE. Uncle Simone, indeed.

LIOLÀ (*to* SIMONE). Come, help me here, Uncle, tell her!

SIMONE *says nothing*.

You too, want to deny it and pin the child on me? Let's be serious, it's you who's ruined her daughter twice, what breed of man are you? A baby with your niece and, within months of conceiving, you make another with your wife. What courses through your veins, the flames of Hell or divine white heat? Mount Etna's soul? God save every mother's daughter within a ten-mile radius of you.

CROCE (*sarcastic*). That's right, we must lock our daughters up against Simone Palumbo.

SIMONE. Liolà, I hoped I wouldn't have to say these things in quite this way, but...

LIOLÀ. What is it, Uncle?

SIMONE. Between myself and Tuzza there never was the sin to which you are referring. She threw herself at my feet, simply, repenting the deed she'd done with you and confessing the state she found herself in. My wife knows everything, I've told her it all. And I am ready to swear to you now, in front of Holy Jesus and the whole village, that Tuzza's is not my baby, I was wrong to say it was. It's yours.

LIOLÀ. So am I now meant to take Tuzza as my wife?

SIMONE. You must, Liolà, because truly the child is yours.

LIOLÀ. You're getting ahead of yourself there, Simone. There was a time when I wanted Tuzza and asked her to marry me, and would have taken her with full heart, but that was then. I did suspect if I married her that the songs might die from my heart, but I'm a romantic. Luckily for me she turned me down, considering who she's revealed herself to be. You can't have a full barrel and a drunk wife, Uncle Simone, Mother Croce, you just can't cut it both ways.

(*To his sons.*) Come on, boys, we're going home.

They turn to go, LIOLÀ *turns back.*

For the sake of my conscience... I see there's one more child than is wanted here – I'm happy to have him.

CROCE. Him?

LIOLÀ. Maybe a girl, there's nothing to inherit so it doesn't matter. Some extra work for my mother, another bed... it's no burden, I'll take him.

TUZZA *storms* LIOLÀ *with* LUZZA'*s knife.*

TUZZA. Take this instead.

Everyone screams. LIOLÀ *stops* TUZZA'*s knife hand just in time.* MITA *faints,* SIMONE *catches her.* LIOLÀ *laughs to reassure everybody.*

LIOLÀ. It's nothing, it's done with. That was close!

He bats TUZZA'*s fingers until she drops the knife, then stands on it firmly.*

Daddy's healthy.

He bends down to kiss one of the BOYS' *heads, reassure him. He notices a line of blood on his chest.*

It's just a graze, look.

He collects some blood on his finger, runs it along TUZZA'*s lips.*

Taste, Tuzzita, sweet, no? Like the sap of a green tree. Can I tell you something, Tuzza? If a bowl is turned upside down, the sun can't shine in to it.

He lets her go, joins his sons, addresses TUZZA.

When he's born, whenever you're ready, bring the baby. I'll teach him to sing. All my children will sing.

He takes his sons by the hand.

(*To* MITA.) Perhaps your child will sing too, Mita. Maybe you'll have more, maybe they'll all sing. All I know is everything perishes save music and love.

Unable to keep some sadness from his voice.

Enjoy your family, Mita.

He heads off with the BOYS. CIUZZA *runs down to catch up with them, walks alongside.* LUZZA *and* NELA *follow at a distance. The* MUSICIANS *start a reprise of 'That's How It Is'. Everyone looks out at us.*

GESA (*singing*).
>Rules are for breaking,
>Life is quite short,
>When your heart's aching
>It's not much sport.

MITA (*singing*).
>Then it all turns with
>Nature's own game

GESA *and* MITA (*singing*).
>You win or you lose
>I've no mind to complain.

THE WHOLE VILLAGE (*singing*).
>That's how it is, that's how it is, that's how it is, how it is, that's how. That's how it is, that's how it is, that's how it is, that's how.

NINFA (*singing*).
>That's how it is.

CROCE (*singing*).
>That's how it is.

TUZZA (*singing*).
>That's how it is.

MITA (*singing*).
>How it is, that's how.

CÀRMINA (*singing*).
>   That's how it is.

SIMONE (*singing*).
>   That's how it is.

LUZZA *and* NELA (*singing*).
>   That's how it is.

CIUZZA (*singing*).
>   How it is.

Beat.

LIOLÀ (*spoken*). That's how.

The End.

www.nickhernbooks.co.uk

 facebook.com/nickhernbooks

 twitter.com/nickhernbooks